'You can be smar[...]
motivational real[...]
their potential, and overcame physical limitations and societal prejudice to build successful businesses. CII congratulates Meera Shenoy for depicting the journey of industry champions who focused on capabilities rather than the disabilities of the differently-abled, created effective businesses and strong brand images for their companies. CII is committed to empowerment of PwDs and promoting as well as enabling mainstreaming within industry. I am confident that these inspirational stories would encourage many more leaders.'

Chandrajit Banerjee, *Director General, Confederation of Indian Industry*

'I am delighted that a very innovative book is being launched. Becoming *smarter and wiser* an aspiration for many and getting guidance from experts who have traversed that path would be of great value. I would strongly recommend this book to every middle manager and entrepreneur.'

Ganesh Natarajan, *Chairman NASSCOM Foundation, Vice Chairman & MD Zensar Technologies*

'It is now well established that the best leaders are those that lead with purpose, inspire and help others be the best they can be. But that is easier said than done except when you read this book. Meera and Prasad have pulled off an amazing set of stories that should be required reading for anyone who is looking for motivation and 'how to's for personal transformation.'

Pramath Raj Sinha, *Founder & Managing Director | 9.9 Mediaworx Pvt Ltd; Founding Dean, ISB; Founder Ashoka University*

'An interesting compilation of motivational real life stories of leaders and entrepreneurs, who are differentially abled or have been supporting employees with disabilities. Each of these stories in the book will inspire us to move beyond our 'comfort zone' and make a difference in our society.'

S. Ramadorai, *Vice Chairman, TCS, Chairman, National Skilling Development Corporation (NSDC)*

'*You Can Be Smarter and Wiser* is a low key title to what is an Inspirational book. It chronicles stories of entrepreneurs and leaders of business and society who have overcome personal challenges to be extraordinarily successful. Much of their success of course originates from their outstanding abilities and leadership qualities, but when set against the constraints of disabilities they had to overcome, their success is amazing; something for all of us to learn from, cherish, and applaud. But that is not all, in the second half of the book, Meera Shenoy and Prasad Kaipa provide instances of forward-looking companies and their leaders making the opportunity for differently abled individuals, that end up with great rewards for the business and the individuals themselves, the classic win-win. It is a fascinating book, with so much to admire and so much to learn from, by absorbing and reflecting on the inspirational stories.'

Prof. V. Kasturi Rangan (Kash Rangan), *Malcolm P. McNair Professor of Marketing, Harvard Business School, Boston, Massachusetts, USA*

'This book offers relevant advice to the business leader of today about the importance of proactively soliciting diverse talent to meet contemporary workforce labour needs. It highlights the importance of nurturing both evident and latent abilities in each of our employees, to assist them in achieving their personal maximum potential and thereby their ability to contribute to bigger picture organizational effectiveness. In this process, the leader doing so will enable efficient use of a wider labour pool of talented individuals, contribute to successful business strategy outcomes, and also deepen their own personal knowledge of the value of true workplace inclusion.'

Susanne M. Bruyère, *Professor of Disability Studies, Director, K. Lisa Yang and Hock E. Tan Institute on Employment and Disability, ILR School, Cornell University, Ithaca, New York U.S.A.*

'This is a book about hope.It is about courage. And courage is contagious. The lived reality of people who have overcome physical and mental challenges inspires us and shows us the way forward in our own lives. We find friendship and support in the pages and know that the world is a better place because the people in the book exist. Their strength will give is strength. A must read.'

Ruchira Gupta, *Professor, New York University and Founder and President Apne Aap Women Worldwide*

'...This book is indeed remarkable for it shakes you up ... out of one's comfort zone and sets you thinking. For there is so much that the society has given us ... isn't it then time to return our bit?'

Pulak Chamaria, *Director; Infinity Group, NGO's : ANANT Education Initiative, Akshaya Patra, Jagriti Dham, JAIPUR Foot, Institute of NEURO Sciences, Institute of Cerebral Palsy*

'This book is a mood elevator'

KV Kamath, *President Brics Bank and Former Chairman ICICI Bank and Infosys*

'...We need mavericks who can evangelize the concept that the specially-abled are superior: that all they need is opportunity and support; that given both, they too can help make the world a better place; that when you see them in the light they need to be seen, they could become potent resources. Which is why this evangelical book You Can: Be Smarter and Wiser needs to be read, comprehended and acted upon. Your time starts now.'

Kolkata Gives-Mudar Patherya, *Jyoti Vardhan Sonthalia, Mukti Gupta, Pawan Agarwal, Anant Nevatia and Saurav Dugar*

'I enjoyed reading this wonderful book. I am impressed with Youth4Jobs challenging but magical work and realise this book is a logical extension. Read and be inspired!'

Amala Akkineni, *Founder, Blue Cross.*

YOU CAN
BE SMARTER AND WISER

YOU CAN
BE SMARTER AND WISER

MEERA SHENOY
PRASAD KAIPA

B L O O M S B U R Y

NEW DELHI • LONDON • OXFORD • NEW YORK • SYDNEY

First published in India 2016

© 2016 by Meera Shenoy and Prasad Kaipa

BLOOMSBURY and the Diana logo are trademarks of Bloomsbury Publishing Plc

ISBN 978 93 854 3661 1
2 4 6 8 10 9 7 5 3

Bloomsbury Publishing India Pvt. Ltd
DDA Complex, LSC Building No.4
Second Floor, Pocket C – 6 & 7, Vasant Kunj
New Delhi 110070
www.bloomsbury.com

Edited by Ruchhita Kazaria

Typeset by Manmohan Kumar
Printed and bound in India by Thomson Press India Ltd.

To find out more about our authors and books visit www.bloomsbury.com. Here you will find extracts, author interviews, details of forthcoming events and the option to sign up for our newsletters.

To the heroic unsung, who quietly work to
make a better world

All the royalty from the sales of this book will go to **Youth4Jobs Foundation,** a not-for-profit organisation which believes in the ability of the disabled. Y4J transforms the lives of youth with disability, especially girls, by training them and linking them to jobs. (www.youth4jobs.org)

Contents

Contents

India has the worlds' largest youth population. The vision of *Skill India* is for everyone; irrespective of caste, creed, gender and vulnerability. It is to realise the potential of these young Indians and for them to acquire the necessary skills for a job or an enterprise.

Our youth need real life role models to inspire them. The entrepreneurs with disabilities potrayed in the first section of this book have persisted against several odds and challenges to achieve their goals. They provide the very role models that our young people seek.

Growing entrepreneurship in India is mirrored by companies seeking sustainable solutions to integrate the have-nots into their work-force. The companies profiled in the second section of this book clearly demonstrate that integrating a vulnerability like disability into the business improves both business metrics and customer satisfaction indexes.

Let us learn from the examples in this book, and all join hands to create several more inspiring models to create a vibrant and inclusive India.

Shri Rajiv Pratap Rudy
Hon'ble Minister for Skill Development & Entrepreneurship

Introduction

All journeys of pioneers are challenging. So too, was my journey with the young men and women with disability. It began three years ago, when I founded Youth4Jobs. The vision was seemingly simple – to reach out to villages for youth, especially girls with disability, build their self-esteem and skills and get them placed them in jobs. I did not anticipate deep mindsets to be the roadblocks on every side. The rural community, including parents, felt their child was not capable of being economically independent. Girls were kept hidden at home, with the persistent fear that their sisters may not get a suitable groom. So, young men and women, who come to our training, have incredibly low self esteem. On the other side, companies actually asked me, 'Will my non-disabled workforce leave, if I hire the disabled?' Our core belief that the poor and vulnerable have latent potential helped us remain focussed. Making this work happen seamlessly, across nine States in eighteen centres, has transformed every young person we touched, economically and socially. It is akin to a miracle. A disabled girl selling flowers on the roadside, despite being a graduate, now works for a media and entertainment company. A young man, who could not get a job even as a village school master is now, employed in a multinational company, after our trainings and campus recruitment services. Parents bless us every day and this helps me deepen and scale up the work.

You cannot do this work without being touched by it. As I speak at forums on how companies can combine compassion with business, which improves their bottom line, I find myself changing – in small ways every day. Being in the act of gratitude to the world – to the forces which help me steer, this challenging but joyful journey.

Conducting research and meeting these incredibly inspiring change agents, entrepreneurs with disability and CEO's who are integrating business with compassion, was part of my journey. Writing their stories is my way of sharing with you, the insight that **everyone can be a change-maker** ... and inviting you to join me, in this journey!

Meera Shenoy – Hyderabad, Telangana, India
Meera.shenoy@gmail.com

Yes, you can – I was told when I was young. Once I started believing in it, I realized that I will and I must. You can too. First my own story:

I grew up in a lower middle-class family in Anantapur; Andhra Pradesh. The best job that I could aspire for, according to my father and his friends, was to become a sub-inspector. But I wanted to be an IAS officer. Despite being intelligent, my problem was a lack of focus. In addition to focus, I had difficulty following through and being self motivated. At that time, I did not know that I have 'Attention Deficit Hyper Issues' which made paying attention on anything for long, a major chore. In school, I fared badly. After finishing school with C average grades, I could barely get into college. Getting a mediocre job was going to be my goal and hope. Then everything changed.

Two teachers – Dr. Rangachari and Mr. Subbarao encouraged me. With this, I developed self belief and gained self confidence. I ended up with first class in B.Sc.; went on to do my Masters and followed up with a Ph.D. from IIT. The rest is history.

Forty years later, I could put my finger on what made the difference to me – they helped me build my psychological capital. Psycap has four elements: Hope, Efficacy, Resilience and Optimism. Together, you can reduce them to an acronym – HERO. That is what my teachers helped me become – a HERO; hopeful, self confident (efficacy), learn from my failures (resilient) and optimistic about the future for me, for you and for the world.

If I could succeed with a mental disability, I believe anybody can do it, wherever they start. For me, it all started because somebody said to me, 'You can, you will and you must!' Now it is our turn to say that to you. You can achieve anything. You can reach your full potential, no matter where you come from and whatever disability you have!

Prasad Kaipa – California, USA
prasad@kaipagroup.com

SECTION 1

I CAN, SO CAN YOU

In each and every one of us, there lies infinite potential. There is a genius, just waiting to be ignited. For some of us, a challenge gets us out of our fears and comfort zones. For others, opportunity makes us entrepreneurs. An insight or a dream can trigger the blossoming of our deeper desires.

Who you are and what you bring to the world is a unique DNA or essence. That essence can be taken for granted. So the skills that we learn through our education or through appreciation that people bestow upon us, are given importance. However, these fade into oblivion and can be classified as insignificant, when compared to the unique, invisible essence that we bring to the world. We become aware of them when we lose them, akin to a death or a divorce. When you tap into this DNA, it clarifies purpose, evokes passion, unleashes power and harvests creativity!

The entrepreneurs featured in this book have 'ignited their inherent genius', thereby making the seemingly impossible, possible. Some perceive them as disabled. But well, they show us they are differently-abled. They are unwilling to buy-in to their limitations or live a life of complaints and misery. They transcend the horizons of their limitations and demonstrate a high degree of creativity, by taking on risks and treading the difficult path. They are not just smart efficient leaders, but rather wise, effective leaders!

You the reader are a unique human being. You may ask how to awaken yourself to this potential of contribution – of capability and realisation within yourself? Read the best practises we present while questioning yourself. Reflect on the excuses you give, for not tapping into your potential. Is it because you are lazy? Or are you content with your degree of being evolved and feel you do not need to make an effort to improve yourself? Read this, thinking of the potential in you, which you are throwing aside saying 'I don't need it'. Remember as a soul, you are here to learn! Realize the wealth which lies hidden in knowledge!

The caterpillar does not become a butterfly for itself. Without butterflies, the world would have fewer flowers. Or without cross pollination, there is no spring.

In this book, we share stories, of both, wise entrepreneurs and leaders. See what you can learn from them. Some stories might remind you of those lessons, which you already know. Take from them – for revision sharpens the saw. And there shall be other stories also, which suggest actions and behaviors that are outside your comfort zone. Read them once and then, slowly, re-read the stories that speak to you and recognize, that you might find lessons, not identified immediately but upon a second and third reading. We would love to hear what you found and what you have done to actualize them in your life.

Ajit Basu

A young start up entrepreneur, with cerebral palsy.

His diminutive frame belies his inner confidence. Diagnosed with cerebral palsy while still in mid-school, Ajit Babu has chosen a path, visibly different from many others with disability. He does not want his disability certificate, for it entitles him to government subsidies; which are immaterial to him. He does not want to settle in with a safe but boring Government job. Instead, his adrenalin rises when he takes risks. Being oblivious to the advice of friends and family, he established an enterprise, while he was all of twenty-six years. Now, he is waiting for his second venture to take off.

Ajit was a premature baby, weighing 1.4 kilograms at birth. It was a herculean task to keep this tiny baby alive and hence, he was kept for two months in the incubator. Ajit got enrolled in a normal school, struggling with all subjects, except English and Kannada. He was excellent when it came to debates and theatre. 'The teachers who had not seen kids with disability, thought that I was lazy not applying myself. Otherwise, how could I be so good in one area and hopeless in the other,' he stated. Those were trying times for him, whenever his parents came to pick him from school. He would pray that they did not meet his teachers. No one understood that young Ajit was trying hard to behave like an equal, like his other non-disabled friends. The grim reality though, was that he was different.

It was only in the seventh standard, that he was diagnosed with cerebral palsy. That he was suffering from dyslexia, was unearthed at the Spastics Society of Karnataka. What followed then, were a series of counselling sessions. Like most parents, who find it difficult to believe that their child has a disability, Ajit's parents could not accept the reality. Once through with his tenth grade, he got pressurised to enrol into PUC. He narrated an incident, when he had failed to clear his paper in accountancy, while in his second year. Though his same age cousins, had however, passed with flying colours. Obviously, it created a storm in his house. His mother was inconsolable, while his father attributed his failure to laziness. Pressure of peers and family kept him plodding on to the path of higher education. He got himself enrolled in college, to pursue psychology, journalism and English Literature. Again, like his school days, he found that he enjoyed journalism and literature, but psychology was not his strong area because of the lab work it entailed. Hence, he began shying from the psychology class. The elders referred to him as 'rebellious'. As a result, young Ajit began shunning family functions, remaining in his room and applying for jobs.

He took up a job in Bengaluru, at a call centre. After quitting there, he joined another call centre and yet another. 'I reach my saturation point soon. It gets monotonous after a point … just saying, "Thank you for calling". Becoming a supervisor takes four to five years. I just felt I could not do it any longer!' He sighed, as he explained his predicament. Exhausted, he decided to leverage his selling skills. For pocket money, he had been supporting his friends in their real estate ventures, working for a commission. He had realized that he was good at it and even enjoyed himself. So he joined Ocwen, a home retention loan company, which provides repayment options to the defaulters. This work was akin to a doctor, for he was saving lives. He invested sixteen hours each day, earning sizeable money and began getting several eMails of gratitude from customers, who had managed to finally buy a home. However, the long hours took a toll on his already frail health and he decided to quit his job.

At this juncture, his father advised him to get a disability certificate from the government and get into a respectable job, using the reservation quota. Ajit however, was clear. 'I wanted no quotas. Reservation does not fix any problem but creates a dependency!' He stated. 'There was a gun on my forehead to settle down, take up a stable job and marry'. Ajit however had other ideas.

Dream Click Concepts, the company he founded, married the two loves of his life – media and selling. Along with a friend, Harish Narayan, he focussed on the company which provided in-film branding. With the idea already popular in Bollywood, they extended the same to Southern cinema. The two partners had complementary skills; Harsh had contacts in the film industry, whereas Ajit was a master at selling. 'This changed my life. The marketing heads of companies would see me – as a thin, weedy chap convincing them that their brand would get enhanced in the film!' He chuckled as he recounted. The company was performing well. However, three years later, they decided to close the company, owing to the unprofessionalism of the film fraternity. They found themselves reneging on the commitments made to various brands. 'I wanted to get out with my company friendships intact,' he rued.

The 3-D printing technology made him feel comfortable with technology, as he looked at its business applications. He flew down to cities like Hyderabad, where institutions like the Engineering Institute, invited him to share his knowledge of the new technology. Simultaneously, the Nepal earthquake happened and he invested his energies into sending solar lamps to the ravaged country. Sitting in a cafe, he saw as usual, several people trying to charge their mobile phones with power banks. The Nepal experience had had him fascinated by the solar technology. He had a simple idea – 'Why not use solar technology to charge the power banks?' Thus, his new company, Lifehack Innovations, was born! Its vision was of integrating renewable energy into ones daily life. 'We look at solar as something expensive and remote. But, can we use this in our daily lives!' became his quest. He soon realised, that the power bank would be more useful if it could be charged from multiple sources – solar, wind and electricity. Raising INR six to seven lakhs from friends, he contracted the research to different technologists, who had a passion for the *jugaad*. While the prototype is now ready, manufacturing requires an investment of INR fifteen lakhs, which he is currently raising. Meanwhile, he is slowly adjusting to the new tune of 'We always knew there was magic in this lad!', as media articles appear about his work. Little do they know that Ajit remembers being criticized by them! 'All my life, I have rebelled against security. It is too boring. A two wheeler and then, two more wheels in a Swift … a wife, two children and a house! Can you live life like that? I don't mind the risks, as it helps me achieve something bigger'. He pauses before he continues, 'I am ambitious! I keep thinking of Tesla; if every start-up can solve one problem of the world, we will leave behind a better place!'

MANTRAS FOR SUCCESS

1. Believe in yourself. In fact, I have a tattoo on my arm with a hash-tag reading 'Believe'.
2. Do not wait for miracles to happen.
3. When you believe in an Idea, put all your efforts into it.

Amit Manga

The one who embodies the spirit of living in the moment!

The para-olympic bronze trophies are proudly displayed in Amit Manga's swanky office, located on the fourth floor of the steel and glass DLF Towers in Delhi. 'A muscle tear prevents me from playing the game now, but I loved the sheer whizzing of the wheel-chairs to play para tennis,' remarks Amit; his eyes twinkling.

Amit wasn't born with any disability; it happened when he was a teen-ager. Disability found him, owing to a delayed medical diagnosis. Today at forty, he runs Perot Enterprises Pvt. Ltd, an INR 8 crore organization, sitting confidently on his wheel-chair. His human-resource strength is twenty-five, of which three have disabilities.

Amit firmly believes in not looking back; drawing strength from the Buddhist adage; 'From this moment on'. This realization and learning has helped him embrace his grim reality with a nod of contentment, both in his personal and professional life.

While a teenager, he was a student of Modern school; Delhi, having a steadfast circle of friends. His family was large, one which had successful entrepreneurs and smart businessmen. When he was nineteen and was playing tennis, one day, he experienced a blinding headache accompanied by a spinning of the head. It was meningitis. However, it was diagnosed too late, taking a toll on his health and well-being. That resulted in a condition called Syringomyelia; which meant that he had been rendered a quadriplegic, with zero sensation of pain or temperature; chest downward. 'My life turned upside down; I had to change gears completely! What was trivial or easy before … was now complex for me, like a person with spinal injuries,' he recounted vividly; his tone surprisingly at ease. Overnight, his life had become a series of scans, hospitalisation and three spinal surgeries. In the beginning for about six years, he walked unsteadily, wobbling around with a stick. Over time, it became rather apparent that he was losing muscle power and motor skills rapidly, which meant that walking would soon be an impossible task.

He had enrolled himself for a two-year International management program in the Fore School of Management. Clutching onto a walking-stick and clambering the stairs was not easy. There were classes on the first floor and as he latched himself on a friends shoulder for support, he found the ordeal to be slow and painful. Once armed with a degree, he began applying for jobs.

A walk down memory lane, Amit shrugged, 'When I spoke to my friends … I learnt that they were all playing my favourite sport – tennis! Moving ahead in different spheres of their respective careers'. Aloof back then, he preferred staying indoors, refusing to have company. Those were dark days indeed. He began questioning the cruel blow of life, isolating himself from the society at large, asking the question, 'Why me?'

As dawn conquered the darkness which had begun engulfing him; there emerged his life-coach, mentor and physiotherapist – Sunil. 'I was pleasantly taken aback! There were young people like me on wheel-chairs playing tennis ... even swimming! It was such a delight that Sunil took me to the stadium ... I saw the players getting in to their cars and driving away,' he smiled, his energy infectious. This interaction gave him a new lease of life. He began exploring the infinite possibilities that surrounded him. Inspiration came in from all quarters. His girl-friend, who is now his wife, also encouraged him to set up a business, since job opportunities were difficult.

His first germ of an idea was advertising, especially because he had been constantly giving jingles to his sister entrepreneur; Geeta Bector. Geeta is a part of the multi-crore Cremica family; one that makes sauces for multi-nationals. He also had an inherent talent for doodling and sketching, but his hands had become shaky.

Amit now concentrated on making a detailed list of the materials, that his family, relatives and friends imported for their respective businesses. Thereafter, he began sending out eMails to the brands and organizations; the key stake-holders, requesting for a dealership. As he took stock of his possessions, all that he could find was a modest sum of INR 10,000 in the bank alongside a computer, bereft of an operator. 'My father being a manufacturer of heavy machinery tools, I didn't want to venture into the same,' he reflected.

Responding to his dealership eMail, the German giant; Bakelite AG made him a distributor. This was the beginning of a luminous journey with the company that made granular powder for switches and auto parts. Believing in the concept of SOHO, he made a small office at home. 'They were intrigued by my introductory eMail and wanted to visit me for a prospective business opportunity. Then they came to Delhi and we met ... well, the rest is history!' I immediately asked, 'Did the Germans hesitate when they saw you perched onto a wheel chair?' 'There wasn't any reaction ... why! None at all,' he winked. But for the first time, he realised that in the world of international business, your ability matters, not your disability.

In hindsight, the timing to become a distributor was perfect. Bakelite had moved out of the Indian territory and there was a demand for the product which still existed. An industrious Amit, found himself setting up dedicated networks by participating in trade fairs. He left no stone unturned to build his business. The results were indeed phenomenal as the volumes rose from 20 tonnes to 5,000 tonnes an year. 'This was a learning curve in my career. Business cannot flourish in the presence of mental barriers. The way the revenues soared ... it was such a morale booster,' he chirped; satisfaction written over all his face.

Every experience was a learning, with something to take-away. For instance, when he was vacationing in Europe, he realized what accessibility really meant. He could travel independently; navigating himself easily through the pavements, roads and buildings alike. This was in sharp contrast to India where most roads and buildings are not accessible. Inevitably, in conferences and meetings, people would quiz him condescendingly, on how he managed his business. Today, Amit runs an INR 8 crore organization, wherein the distribution is centralised alongside the streamlined inventory and processes. Effectively leading a core group of twenty-five staff, he remains the sole distributor for Bakelite since the last 14 years.

In recent years, business has become competitive with cheaper substitutes from China and elsewhere. This has propelled Amit to initiate a discussion with the multinational, to set up a manufacturing unit in India itself, in a bid to lower the production cost. Simultaneously, he has begun assisting his eighty-year old father in his work. There is a generation gap, he admitted, but quite often, the wisdom of his father prevails. The bright side of it is that he gets to travel more often on work. 'Travel, apart from being a stress-buster, also opens my mind to new possibilities'.

A constant encourager around him is his life-partner; Tina. 'Our partnership goes long back, when she was all of sixteen and I was but eighteen. When I had learnt about my health, I had voiced my apprehensions to her quite clearly. As destiny had planned it, she did not relent under family pressure and stood by me, as a rock support. She's made me do everything I could ... except bungy jumping!' He laughs, pausing to steal a glance at a photograph, mounted on the wall. 'We are a lovely family and we have a seven-year old son!'

Buddhism and spirituality provides him with the indispensable inner strength. 'I have realised what is absolute happiness and relative happiness. This has made me humble.

It has instilled in me a degree of compassion for all beings. And most importantly, it has helped me discover my ability in my disability!' He concludes, as he wheels his way out of the office, stepping into his modified Audi, ensuring the middle path between his work and home.

MANTRAS FOR SUCCESS

1. Be practical.
2. Believe in your conviction.
3. Stay with it no matter what. Your time will come

Anand Kulkarni

Reel made more real:

A real life story of Anand Kulkarni; one who makes movies without being able to see them!

His business card is rather intriguing. It reads 'Anand Kulkarni; Right Brain'. Further down, it reads – 'Flop Films, Hungry Foolish Creative'. All of twenty-four, Anand is a writer, editor and film director. Well, and that's not all … to add to the phenomenal quotient, he happens to be almost completely blind.

To me, he came across as a captivator! His questions never ceased to amaze and so did his brutal honesty, coupled with his cheekiness. Like Jiddu Krishnamurti, he fiercely questions everything which surrounds him, with the conviction that the solutions must and have to emerge from oneself. Whether one could dub him as curious, inquisitive or someone who plays the devil's advocate is a matter of choice. But I was clearly fascinated by his outlook towards life.

Soon afterwards, we found ourselves exchanging warm smiles

over a cold coffee, as we sat at the Starbucks cafe at Oberoi Mall, Mumbai. My head was brimming with a flurry of questions. To begin with, how could he 'see' emotions? How did he know that precise moment to say 'cut' in a high-pitch, clear tone? I had seen directors at work earlier and their squint followed by a crisp 'cut' still resonated in my ears. As the mute questions managed to find my voice, he smiled. His smile which was rather infectious. 'It's simple! I make a guarantee each time.' He paused ere he chuckled, 'I guarantee a flop each time, to each of my client. Then, if it's a success … isn't that great?' This explained the name of his organization – 'Flop Films, Hungry Foolish Creative'.

If one scratches beneath the surface of his flippant nature, one shall find its nothing save a mask. For beneath the surface, dwells a focussed approach. Anand specialises in the niche yet, growing arena of digital entertainment. His client base speaks of advertising agencies alongside consumer goods companies. His mentor list has the ace actor Naseeruddin Shah, who got persuaded by Anand and his 'hare-brained' ideas.

Anand, though he was born with regular vision is 80 per cent blind today. It all began while he was in his second year at school. His eyesight began giving grave issues. Tests conducted revealed that he too, was suffering from a rare macular degeneration, like his elder brother. The family was based out of Nagpur. It was then that his father took a life-changing decision of relocating to Mumbai. Disability needed reasoning and response from teachers in schools, which would be better available in Mumbai as compared to Nagpur. 'This sacrifice on his part really paid off!' Anand smiled, as he retold the life incident; his countenance happy.

With Mumbai being more inclusive in its approach, it wasn't long that Anand and his sibling adapted to their new school environment. 'Maturity and rationale comes early, if you are disabled,' he explained. Amongst his first lessons to himself, was this – 'One needs to find solutions, to exist and educate oneself!' In the Geometry class, when the mentor spoke about the three sides of a triangle, it was indeed difficult for him to fathom the same. The only child in his class with failing vision, he needed someone to explain the concept, whilst he drew it correctly. The need of the hour was patience and persistence – be it at school or back home.

'The system also does not always support disability,' he gives a life pointer. He had various friends coaching him on different subjects. During the Board examination, the authorities however, declared that he would have to stick to the same writer for all subjects. There were no computers, scanners, softwares or technology which assisted those with low vision. Yet, Anand topped the special category in class XII by scoring an envious 88 per cent. His father was keen on him studying Commerce, for Anand's elder brother was then in Stanford, for his degree in MBA. Anand, however, had different plans – He wanted to pursue Arts and hence, gave an ultimatum to his father – to allow him to study arts or he would sit at home. Anand enrolled himself in a mass media course with a heady subject-mix of Sociology, Media Research, Advertising and Understanding Cinema. He had effectively sown the seeds of his future career. He recounted a project or two as we sat at the cafe – For his Sociology class, he had to make a short film; wherein he captured the life of the *pan-wallahs*. The other project was converting a poem into a film. Anand found that he enjoyed the process and this was his calling. His father was sceptical as the field was competitive, needing ample resources; his son clearly had a handicap.

Kayoze Irani, son of Boman Irani once told him, 'You have got it in you … to tell stories. Forget competition, just go ahead!' Constant encouragement from his friends nurtured his talent alongside his fierce determination. 'When I told my father that I had plans to go professional … he thought it was a phase. One that would last for six months before I got back to the pedestrian path,' he grinned.

The first venture; titled, 'The Lens Flare Project' was a social one. The idea behind it was – Could different creative minds come together and help the Non-Governmental Organisations (NGO) communicate their message? 'When I looked at the NGO's, I learnt that while some did the good work, they went unnoticed. Those who won the awards had marketed themselves well; hence Lens Flare.' Different themes of the NGO's were handled differently, according to the focus area of their work. Child rights or cleanliness were handled creatively – Organising painting shows, theatre productions with celebrities and likewise. Events like chat shows with the youth, to understand policies, had youngsters asking frank and yet at times, troublesome questions to the policy-making *babus*. While many youngsters acted as the devil's advocate and asked blunt questions, innovative ideas also got generated alongside, which the government could then explore. Realising the power of this idea, he even met the Deputy Chief Minister of Maharashtra, to request his help to take the project to the masses. Ajit Pawar eventually did give a letter of support. Next, he convinced Naseerudin Shah to host and mentor theatre actors' participation. Reliving a memory, he narrated, 'Naseer Sahab is a noted perfectionist – one who gives a single take! However, on one occasion, I felt that I needed to take a second shot. So I said that unhesitatingly. After a ten second dead silence, the stalwart agreed!' The Lens Flare project sadly did not scale up. 'Not because it wasn't doable … but because I did not have the requisite experience to run an organization. A college festival is different from doing a business!' admitted Anand frankly.

While incorporating Flop Films, he was clear that he did not require an MBA or attend a film school. 'No one in a live school has the time or patience to tell me how to understand lighting,' he observed, while rendering an example. This led to him evolving in his own ways with techniques to understand the nuances of the visual world.

Curiosity has people thronging to him with questions. 'They ask a lot of questions. Like how do I comprehend the emotions of the protagonist or whether everything is in focus. Actually, while at work, I tend to ask a lot more questions. I also use audio and intuition as a measure to evaluate!' he elucidates. While he cannot see the monitor, he can give detailed instructions on how to set the light for different shots. An advantage, he admits, is having a team which has become his spine. Kuldeep; Director of Photography, has worked on several acclaimed films like 'Haider' and 'Ship of Theseus' amidst others. Anand sums up the bonding, 'Both of us connect at a thought level. I suppose the very fact that he works with me … means something!'

These days, Anand can be witnessed focussing on a niche

area of digital advertising, one that is online and application based. 'When I working on the Allen Solly brand in 2013, I got hooked onto the instant feedback from the audience. What a lovely, new kind of communication this is,' he gushed. Since the feedback is instant, the director has to convey the message quicker; unlike a television shot, there is no luxury of time. The big story is there but it has to be put into smaller bits and then, the feedback is instant. He did a music video with Raghu Dixit and 'Content & Promos' for a range of clients like Harley Davidson, Johnny Walkers and Ogilvy. While advertising brings in the money, it is the documentaries which continue to be a fascination. He did a thirty minute off-beat documentary on correctional homes which tells stories of the prison staff working there and shows jails are not just a sad place as is the general public perception. 'This permission business is quite weird with regards to documentaries. One needs scores of permissions to shoot … and then, there is no permission to take the same to the masses, the audience!' he states.

The world of media is fast changing and forever in a flux. Though Anand prefers having end-to-end control on the entire process of writing, editing and executing the film, these days he writes less, as the script is written by the specialists. As he dreams of taking Flop Films onto a national level; a nascent project that he has been working on quietly, is to make available online, the e-commerce of the film making process. With his tenacity, resilience and the incredible way in which he brings alive everything that he cannot even see … his journey can only be adjudged as a successful saga.

MANTRAS FOR SUCCESS

1. Parents never calm down at whatever stage you are. They are parents.
2. Find someone, who believes in you a little more than you believe in yourself. Then hang on to his coat tails.
3. Find the 'Why' of you wanting to do something! The 'How' and 'What' shall follow.

On a wheel chair, he has mastered the art of converting losses to profits.

Business pundits describe him as the 'Turn-around Man'. Arvind Verma took over an ailing business that was running at a reported loss of INR 1.5 crores. Today, the same company employs 800 people with a turn-over of INR 316 crores. 'My employees are the backbone of this success.' he says with a hint of pride, as he steers his wheel-chair to welcome me, at his residence in East Kailash; New Delhi.

Arvind was like any other youngster – active in sports and outdoor activities. When he was fourteen, while on a holiday with his friends, in the failing light of the day, he rushed towards what he thought was a short-cut. Alas! There wasn't any short cut. Instead, he tumbled down a precipice and broke his spine. The doctors gave their verdict – Arvind; now a paraplegic, was not to walk again!

His first thought, he voiced, was that he could no longer play golf. His mother was obviously crestfallen but the young Arvind realised that the power to live was in his hands. He then reasoned with his mother that he was trying to climb a few steps; that if she kept crying he would fall down again. His mother, hearing those wise words, took a resolution of standing by his side, through his journey of life.

His parents decided to invest their savings in his recovery, thereby sending him to Stoke Mandeville Hospital; Aylesbury, UK. It was known for the rehabilitation of war veterans. The National Spinal Injury Centre of UK was located in this hospital. The rehabilitation schedule was rigorous and involved an arm strengthening regime by archery, swimming and physiotherapy, since the legs were not functional. Every day was a challenge, with every activity leaving him in tears. Yet, in ninety days, with lessons in self-management, he rejoined his school and worked hard, to catch-up on the year he had missed out on. The school authorities extended support and co-operation, by even shifting the science laboratory onto the ground floor.

The first taste of discrimination came during his college years at St. Stephen's College. The head of Macro-Economics insisted that he only took classes on the first floor and did not want to admit Arvind. 'I was at a loss of words ... I didn't want to be rejected just because I had limited mobility,' he reflected; sorrow apparent from his tone. For months together, he pushed himself up the stairs, to attend the class on time. One day, the unimagined transpired – the professor opted for the class to be shifted to the ground level. Grinning, he remarked, 'So, behaving normal, not complaining and being positive about your abilities help!' This learning has remained with him, through the journey of life.

Arvind completed his Chartered Accountancy and worked for four years with Price Waterhouse Coopers (PWC). In the beginning, his superiors hesitated to give him work, until he protested and requested to be sent out on audit, like the others. His first assignment was Ballarpur Industries at Yamuna Nagar. Thereafter, there was no looking back and he got himself onto the merit list, at the London headquarters with a promising career ahead. That was the precise time, when he decided to take a leap, almost akin to a gamble.

His father was a director in AIMIL (Associated Instruments Manufacturing India Limited), which manufactured and distributed specialised instruments. The management had decided to sell a manufacturing unit because of the rising problems being posed by the Union. Young Verma, who sat through the financial negotiations, felt that the price being offered by the buyer was far low. His father was startled when he offered to buy the company. He was worried as Arvind had no engineering background and even made his stand clear, that the family had no ancestral money to squander. The PWC heads also told Arvind to take a year off, which the company would treat as an industrial experience. 'I realized then, that I must burn my boats with no safety net!' So at twenty-four years, he told his father that he no longer had a job.

There were several challenges. 'When people underestimate your abilities, you end up performing better!' The workers could not accept a youngster on a wheel-chair as their leader. The union leaders began using crude language as a way to defy the decision. However, the rage and rowdiness died down following an incident of Arvind's firm-handedness with a muscle-man. To add to the ado, the finances of the company were in an absolute mess, as the previous management had focused only on good technical people, thereby neglecting the other indispensable aspects. Arvind restructured the unit: cost-cutting across various arenas without compromising on quality. For instance, he began outsourcing work to ancillaries, owned and run by entrepreneurs among the workers. He provided them with a bank limit and asked each of them to employ ten others in turn. All of them being tough Sardars, no documents were signed. 'Thirty-five years later, they remain to be our most successful ancillaries. Some of the workers now have two cars, with a turnover of 3 crores. It's a win-win for the management and the worker turned entrepreneur'.

Having turned the factory in Mathura road around and ensuring its smooth-sailing for over five years, he took over the distribution business, beginning with the Delhi office. When he was asked to deal with the Calcutta union, he took over the region and was aptly labeled as a 'trouble-shooter'. When the Southern and Western distributors wanted to leave, to start a dotcom company, he began staying three weeks a month in Bangalore; gaining a country-wide grip on the distribution business. 'There were, of course, difficulties. I remember in Calcutta, they wanted to shift me from a wheel-chair to a cane chair. It was an old airbus. They carried me up the stairs and pushed me on the seat. No one was bothered to heed to my request and give me an aisle. I looked up and saw the food packets marked – Mumbai. They had put me on a Mumbai bound aircraft rather than Delhi!' He recalled yet another incident at the International airport, where the security person told him in Hindi, to stand up. When Arvind expressed his inability to do so, the security guard retorted, 'Then why are you not on a stretcher?' Adding injury to insult, he looked at the urinal bag and remarked, 'Taang utha ke bataiye' (Lift your legs and show this). Arvind's traveling was extensive and by himself. Such incidents undoubtedly left his mother and sister upset. Arvind however, was made of a different mettle. Deep within his soul, he made peace with the thought that people like the security guard were not to be blamed – for they were essentially ignorant about disability and inclusion.

On the business front, new opportunities materialised through sheer persistence. For instance, India was not known as a quality manufacturing country; with exports being limited. He was determined to get orders from ELE; their single largest competitor. So he knocked at their door, every year in UK. After ten years, the new President asked him if the company could make compressors at a certain price. Today, that small opportunity has grown to be a 100 per cent export factory, dedicated to contract manufacture. They have joint ventures with an American and a German company, which utilizes them as a manufacturing hub for South East Asia and China.

Health issues still persist. Seven years back, the pain in his back was diagnosed as Tuberculosis of the spine, for which he underwent a thirteen hour surgery, in UK. Six months later, the pain resurfaced, with the doctors exclaiming that the impossible had happened – Tuberculosis had attacked the spine again. 'I'm told that my spine is not stable … but I'm not ready for a surgery,' he reflects. He feels that the educated masses need to change their attitude towards the disabled. 'The uneducated speak out on your face but if you explain, they do listen'. This reinstates his conviction that it is the educated society, which is worse. When he wanted to swim at the club, the attitude of those around was amazing. 'Though my breast-stroke and back-stroke exceeds the speed levels required for the Paralympics, there were these elitists around me, sniggering. I felt like reminding them that disability is not contagious!' He laughed at he recounted the unpleasant experience.

The physical state does not dampen his spirit to scale his business to newer levels. The company slogan – 'Beyond Options. Solutions' reflects his personal philosophy. He has already succeeded in changing the image of AIMIL from conservative, to one which is willing to take risks, believing in the cutting edge of technology. The focus now, is on diversification to reduce the risks. Arvind believes that he offers a competitive advantage to his principals, to shift their manufacturing to India as compared to China. Indians have the advantage of English language, deep technical expertise with a 'Jugaad' attitude and a legal system that functions well. In-keeping with the disadvantages of poor infrastructure and unethical business practices, the company has diversified into consultancy and training also. Future plans include setting up of a foundation, which nurtures varied talents, including re-tooling loyal, retired workers who have the knowledge wealth and the expertise goodwill. 'These retired workers have lived and breathed AIMIL and mere age should not make them redundant', he says. A novel concept indeed!

MANTRAS FOR SUCCESS

1. Cultivate a positive attitude.
2. Be committed to your goals and acquire the right tools.
3. Everyone is born with a potential – once you have realized it, nurture it.

Bhavna Bhotta

Born with cerebral palsy, she dreamt of becoming an entrepreneur!

Tucked away in the quiet lanes of Srinagar colony; Chennai, close to the Vinayaka temple is a board – 'Sahaayadri'; the abode of Ahimsa silk. Step into the spacious room and the shelves are lined with myriad colours of Jharkhand, Andhra and Chhattisgarh weaves. All of twenty-seven years, Bhavna, the founder-owner is wheeled in. Having non-verbal cerebral palsy, all her communication is through the eyes. She understands and speaks English, Tamil, Telugu and Hindi. With grit and determination, coupled with a supportive family, she has not allowed her disability cripple her entrepreneurial dreams. Our conversation is unusually delightful, with her eyes expressing the joys of being economically independent.

Her mother, Kalpana, recalls that in the maternity hospital at Vijayawada, she had realised that the baby's nails were becoming blue. Later, she was told that a gash on the baby's forehead, due to a forcep delivery, had led to the seizures and unusual health problems. Exhaustive rounds of meeting different doctors ensued, yet the problem was not diagnosed until little Bhavna was six months old. 'We had never heard the term before – cerebral palsy!' says Kalpana, 'till Dr. Kamala, who has been our main guiding force, gave us this shocking verdict. The doctor advised us to read rhymes and books to her, like one would to a normal child'.

'Vidya Sagar; my school and its director; Ms. Rajul taught me to look at life differently!' She uses an augmentative and attentive communication system, which is customised to her requirements. It is an eye-pointing technique, enabling a person to view a chart that displays letters or words, alongside signs for yes and no. She also uses a 'Smart Navigator', which is similar to an infrared *bindi*. It catches her head, hand and eye movement, thereby allowing the alphabets to get typed onto a computer screen. 'One can even Skype using it!' She gushes, rather excitedly. The Tamil Nadu State Board gave her special permission to give her examinations, using this eye-pointing technique, since computer print-outs are not allowed. However, the technique causes tremendous strain on her eyes. Kalpana; a proud mother, her voice choked, reflects, 'Bhavna is a fighter! She had no intentions of giving up. Years just went by and she was in College'.

Bhavna had sown the seeds of her entrepreneurial dreams, while in college. While studying for her commerce degree, she had set up a stall, displaying products made by disabled groups. Moving from a sheltered school like Vidya Sagar; where her mother was the Principal to Lady Andal and Ethiraj College, where she was the only student with profound disability, was not an easy task. However, destiny was kind as she found support systems in her mentors and her friends at large. Sporting a smile, she recounted, 'They absolutely adored me! My class-mates went out of their way to make me comfortable ... while the mentors made adaptations in the classroom for me'.

Bhavna wanted to pursue an MBA, but education had taken a toll on her health. She then decided to begin with a home venture. Every evening, supported by her younger sister; Nandini, she would pitch various ideas to the family before dinner. Finally, they narrowed their options and decided upon eco-friendly silk. Her understanding with her parents was clear – She was averse to being funded by them. With her care-giver, she visited the nearby Indian Overseas Bank, enquiring about loan application for women entrepreneurs. The auditor and scribe reasoned with her to take a partner on-board, for signing cheques and doing allied activities. However, she was resolute that she could do it herself! The permissions took time and every morning at nine, when the bank shutters opened, Bhavna would be there on her wheel-chair demanding when she could draw the money.

Like all first generation entrepreneurs, Bhavna too, learnt by making mistakes. Her suppliers and weavers did not believe in deadlines, leading to money getting blocked, which the fledging business could ill-afford. Other suppliers were in remote areas, which were not accessible by wheel-chair.

Finally on 3rd September 2011, *Saahaagika* (meaning 'Natural') was inaugurated in her house. She pegs it as a business with a social conscious. As a WWF (World Wildlife Fund) member and PETA (People for Ethical Treatment of Animals) activist, she was troubled to learn that 2,600 silkworms were sacrificed to roll out one pound of traditional silk. Hence, she decided to stick to the eco-friendly, *'ahimsa'* path. Her stocks include organic silk from 'Jharkand Silk Textiles and Handicrafts Corporation'; a Government of Jharkhand undertaking, which gives her commission on sales. She also sources from Kusuma Rajaiah; the pioneer with a patent in 'Ahmisa Silk'. The process is long and time consuming, for the silk is woven from the cocoons, only after the silkworms turn into moths. In the absence of pesticides and chemicals, the silk gets softer with each wash. Her profitability is client-satisfaction along-with a small mark-up of 20 per cent. 'They all appreciate her will-power ... which helps Sahaayadri develop a loyal customer base!' dotes her mother. To simplify her work and reduce the inventory, she has moved into e-commerce using the Shopify platform. Apart from helping her to reach out to a wider market and keep up with the modern marketing techniques, the online medium also allows her ample time. 'I get ample time to do things I enjoy – Like taking part in dharnas!' She grins. Her work done with will power and grit has made her a CavinKare Mastery awardee, given to achievers with disability.

She is an active member of the Disability Rights Alliance, whose members are passionate about advocacy for disability issues, like the changes in the recent Disability Bill. She actively participates in their monthly meetings. She also meets the alumni of Vidya Sagar School, now part of a youth club, where they discuss their challenges and joys. 'My activist daughter is quite a media figure,' gushes Kalpana ere she continues, 'When the policemen came for her passport verification recently, one of them remarked that he knew her well, as he had seen her in dharnas and in meetings with the Governor'.

Bhavna plans to take a break, to join her sister in the United States for three months. It was Bhavna after all, who had proudly funded her younger sister's ticket to the States for higher education. Undeterred by any challenges she plans her next venture – a cosy coffee shop, resembling a book-store and boutique! In the interim, she combines business with attending the PETA, WWF and other meetings in Chennai, discussing at length issues close to her heart. She believes in living life king-size, which she described as 'simply like any other young woman'.

MANTRAS FOR SUCCESS

1. Do not fear solitude – It can be empowering
2. Do not hesitate to take help, but learn to try independently
3. Cultivate a passion apart from business. It nurtures the soul.

Divya Arora

She combines two seemingly different worlds of disability and entertainment!

She is India's first wheel-chair theatre activist, writer-actor in celluloid cinema and one of the winners in the recent Miss India Wheel-Chair beauty pageant. Dressed in soft hues of pink, with silver hands, fingers and toes; her elfin charm and resilience left me speechless.

Who has not admired Hrithik Roshan for his flawless performance as a quadriplegic in *Guzaarish*? The person behind his perfect acting was none other than Divya Arora, who was hand-picked by Sanjay Leela Bhansali. Her large, expressive eyes twinkling, she mentioned that her next project – 'Pyar Actually', is a full-length commercial feature film; written, acted and directed by her. She has given the script to Nagesh Kukanoor, the well know film actor/director. Knowing his penchant for unusual subjects, she is confident of his affirmative nod.

'I entertain on a wheel-chair to show the world; especially India, that we are not mere commodities.

So when I prepare a theatre production, I expect people to pay and laugh with me … not laugh at me!' Divya's firm conviction is that theatre is a powerful tool, to raise awareness of issues pertaining to disability. Her first brush with theatre was while presenting and acting in the adaptation of 'Bare foot in the Park' by Neil Simons, on World Disability day. The play is a two hour romantic comedy, revolving around a lawyer and his free-spirited wife. Next on the cards was the play 'Melody of Love'; an eighteenth century French play, written by the French playwright; Marivaux, which formed a part of her Master's thesis. Having lived in London and Paris during her formative years, she is multi-lingual. She is proficient in French, Japanese and Nepali, besides English and Indian dialects. On one occasion, she discovered that the play had been translated into 72 languages, sans English. That is how her journey began – with her quick translation, applying for copyright and staging the production. While she herself acted as Princess Sylvia; Tom Alter played her father and R.J. Mantra, her lover. Since its first performance in 2001, the play has travelled all over the country. Celebrities like Priyanka Chopra have been invited as the chief guests. 'The funds go to a cause … but the main message behind these productions is to stir the public … the theatre and the film fraternity. We are no different than those with abilities!'

Ironically, she was born without any disability. However, call it destiny or severe neglect by the doctor that she became a white baby with parts of the brain (those responsible for motor activity) not getting sufficient oxygen. This led to cerebral palsy, rendering her wheel-chair bound for life. 'If this had happened abroad, we could sue the doctors … but in India, one can just feel helpless!' she rued. Her parents encouraged her to be independent, which proved to be a turning point in her life. Her early years in Paris, London and the United States of America were easier, because of the accessibility coupled with the sensitivity of the people. Coming back home to Delhi, and now Mumbai, has made Divya realise how important it is to educate people about disability. Her choosing theatre is aimed at communicating this aspect of disability to those around. Quite rightly, she felt, theatre was a better tool of communication than preaching or giving long sermons.

Divya said she eats, breathes and sleeps theatre but lives film. She met Sanjay Leela Bhansali while he was planning Guzaarish. She recounted that the director was instantly mesmerised by her energy on the wheel chair; exclaiming that he had found the right person. As he went on to narrate the plot, he enquired if she would come on board. 'I didn't know who the star was! Though a star for me is an ordinary person with extra talent. Someone whom the masses worship!' Obviously, she leapt at the opportunity as it would provide her with a footing into the world of cinema. Initially, she was bombarded with research questions like – 'What does injury to the spine at the fourth or the third level mean?' Later, when she was required on the sets, she shifted her base from Delhi to Mumbai. She spent several private moments with Hrithik Roshan, helping him understand the nuances of eating and sleeping on a wheel-chair. 'I made him understand helplessness … How to place his hands, since he cannot remove a fly sitting on his nose!' She elucidated. She even made him fall twenty-five times, till he perfected the act.

Another talented film director, that she was associated with, is Anurag Kashyap. Once again, she was entrusted with explaining the nuances of disability, for his much acclaimed film 'Barfi'. A mega hit at the box-office, it had the star cast of Ranbir Kapoor and Priyanka Chopra; both of whom were persons with disability in the film.

To keep her home-fire burning, Divya works as a Creative Associate in Cine Yug; a company owned by the Malpanis. Despite her wide repertoire, the role of an actor or rendering a voice-over isn't easily awarded – especially to a disabled. With her mantra being – 'Never Say Die!' she has invested in an agent who markets her quite effectively. She has won several awards, including the prestigious Karmaveer Puraskar, in the civil society category. She recounted that Sanjay Dutt; the Bollywood actor was to hand over the Dr. Batra's Positive Health Award to her. Sanjay, being a sensitive person, broke down, weeping inconsolably. 'I had to tell him … can you please stop crying and hand me the award?' she chuckled as she spoke.

'My dream now is to be the first person on a wheel-chair to do the screen play, scripting, dialogues and lyrics of a full-length feature film,' she elucidated. Since her hands are deformed, it takes her longer, as compared to others, to type using a computer. In fact, the script took her two long years, as the nights witnessed her burning the midnight oil. 'But you see … it's not impossible!' There shines her indomitable spirit. When asked about the film, she shared – 'It's typically Bollywood. A romantic comedy which will of course, incorporate disability. My lifelong aim is to mainstream a cause that is real to me. I intend making cinema and entertainment meaningful'. Echoing her life goals, she hurried away to rehearse for her upcoming theatrical production.

MANTRAS FOR SUCCESS

1. Just go for it.
2. Never, ever stop dreaming.
3. Never let disability overshadow your ability.

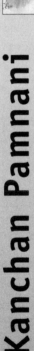

Kanchan Pamnani

They say, 'Justice Is Blind' – A blind lawyer proves it.

Her energy and joi de vivre makes anyone forget that she is blind. Her father, a lawyer himself, dissuaded her from joining the legal profession, in keeping with her failing vision. Kanchan, however, was resolute. Realizing her obstinacy and dedication, he altered his decision and supported her whole heartedly. Their encouragement resulted in Kanchan becoming the proprietor of Pamnani & Pamnani; a firm of advocates and solicitors, operating out of Colaba; Mumbai. Her clients include Indian multinationals, non-resident Indians, private and public trusts alongside high net-worth individuals. When I asked her if law is a good profession for the visually impaired, she asked in rhetoric, 'Lady Justice herself is blind. What better profession could I choose?'

Her current portfolio, a mix of pro-bono disability work and commercial work, keeps her as busy as a bee. She has several feathers in her cap, including two landmark cases of National impact and importance. In Maharashtra, students with visual impairment could not take a scribe (One who writes for the blind during the examinations, as the answers are dictated). A Public Interest Litigation was filed in the Hon'ble High Court, requesting a proper process of ascribing scribes be put in place and an extension of time to complete the examination papers. Kanchan remembers standing outside the court with the NGO's and writing these guidelines, thereafter presenting this disability perspective to the court with suitable arguments. 'The policy was accepted by the State Government but more importantly, the National guidelines were drafted using this work as the base,' her voice resonated with satisfaction and pride.

The other case was getting the Reserve Bank of India (RBI) and the Indian Bankers Association to develop detailed guidelines, listing all possible facilities which visually impaired could have access to. The same included – mobile banking, internet banking, demat amidst other services. 'Here I not only helped to draft exhaustive guidelines, but adopted a "Munnabhai" approach – That of hounding the Chief General Manager of RBI, with every problem that cropped up'. From 2010, she has been working with Krutika; a 12th standard visually impaired student, who had trouble enrolling into the paramedical course. 'The advantage of winning a battle for one person like Krutika, who is now doing her four and half years paramedical course, is that a precedent has been set. Now, the adaptation in the course structure for a visually impaired student shall get streamlined,' she explains. While the disability pro-bono cases give her tremendous satisfaction, her bread and butter comes from the commercial cases.

Her work is a mixture of off and in-court cases. For example, in her law firm, she handles drafting of wills also. This is done by drafting the probate, which is aimed at settling the property without any family quarrels. 'Akin to a family doctor, I become the family lawyer. The position calls for complete trust.' Initially, while arguing in the court, she used to miss witnessing the facial expressions of the Judge, the raised eyebrows of the opposing counsel and the non-verbal body language nuances of others. But today, everyone in the court accepts her as a blind lawyer and she too, has become sensitive to picking up cues in myriad unusual ways!

The transition from a life of surgeries – childhood cataract, squint, nystagmus, retina degeneration and macular degeneration, to becoming a successful legal entrepreneur has not been kind. While in school, she had to use 'Memorex' and other methods to remember what she had heard; a strategy aimed at compensating for her limited vision. 'My mother taught me mathematics with matchsticks on the dining table,' she reminisced. She excelled at debates and won several competitions, which helped build her self-esteem.

After a degree in Commerce from Syndenham College, she decided to do her LLB. Her father and her eye specialist were both startled when they learnt about her decision to follow her fathers' footsteps and be a lawyer. They tried reasoning with her, but to no avail. Realising that she was adamant, her parents supported her by buying different study lamps, magnifying glasses and strange eye-glasses, which would supplement her failing vision. Alongside, they took her to various surgeons, including overseas. Gradually, the failing eyesight turned to absolute blindness. But her grit and determination to become a lawyer, was not deterred by any of these challenges. She not only completed her LLB and LLM at the Bombay Hight Court, but even went on to complete a Qualified Lawyers Transfer Test (Solicitor; Supreme Court of England), from The Law Society; England. For her, moving from low-vision to no-vision was moving from uncertainty to certainty. At the age of 34, she was completely blind and had to build a world around this!

Have clients left her when they realize she is blind? 'Well, sometimes, large firms halve their fees ... despite giving a competent report,' she admits. However, in most cases, since her clients come through referrals, they are aware of her blindness and do not find any difference in the level of professionalism. But that does not rule out the frustrations, which do crop up at times. 'So, in the face of even a typo mistake, it is not attributed to a human error or clerical mistake ... but rather, is pegged to my disability. Perfection is the only way ahead and yes, it is overwhelming at times,' she added. Technology is a boon these days. She can read all the documents using the JAWS reading software, except for the handwritten and scanned documents, where she relies on volunteers reading out the literature aloud. But, despite all the technological advances, the simplest things like flipping through a forty pager document cannot be done by a blind person. 'I have become overweight!' She rues, 'Where is the time to exercise? My time is spent perfecting my work. Further, I'm not good at billing, so friends give me large chocolate boxes from the Taj'. She laughs, letting me get an insight to her sweet-tooth and admitted that she hoped to organise her life, in a bid to shed these extra kilos.

Indeed, life is not all work and no play for Kanchan. She holds a diploma in speech and drama from the Trinity College of Music. She has studied photography and exhibited her shots on many occasions. She is also an ardent lover of Bollywood films and theatre. She has travelled extensively, by herself, in the United States and Europe, realizing that accessibility here is much more sorted than in India. 'Look at the pot holes, puddles and incessant hawkers on the roads here. Commuting is so difficult,' she reflects, though not in a complaining manner.

Kanchan believes in the power of knowledge and hence, never loses an opportunity where she can learn. This renders her the competitive edge. She has recently completed two courses on the Internet – On Intellectual Property Law, conducted by the World Intellectual Property Organisation; Geneva. Her work has won several awards like the Neelam Kanga Award, given by the National Association of Blind and the Cavin Kare Award, given by Ability Foundation. She grew up reading Perry Mason and modelled on her hero. She is striving to use her legal acumen to work on social injustices, in a bid to leave behind a world with equal opportunities!

MANTRAS FOR SUCCESS

1. Work hard and persist on your chosen path.
2. Do not be overly sensitive.
3. Knowledge is the greatest power – keep acquiring it.

Nipun Malhotra

'It's attitudes that disable,' says the young entrepreneur; Nipun, from a wheel chair.

Sitting in the atrium of the Indian School of Business with twenty-eight years old Nipun Malhotra, I realize that his infectious energy is rubbing onto me. It is indeed difficult to fathom that this cheerful persona is wheel-chair bound, suffering from a rare congenital disease – Arthrogryposis. This disease inhibits any muscle growth in his limbs.

Nipun was attending a course on family business with other youngsters; all making plans to scale their businesses in novel ways. It is then, that he remarked, 'I leverage my strength, which is strategy in business. With a team of consultants, I have drawn up a five year growth path for Nipman Fastners; a business started by my father. We make automotive fasteners for bikes and automotive vehicles. I intend to make this into one of India's largest conglomerates'.

His early days were indeed lonely. Instead of going to a

kindergarten, he made rounds of hospitals for corrective surgeries. When he was ready for school, at the age of five, no school was ready to admit a child with disability. His parents were advised to send him to a special school, equipped at handling differently abled children. But Priyanka, his mother, had vowed that he would live life like any other child. He was finally admitted to St. Marys School, where he excelled in mathematics; calculating in his head rather than on paper. He remembers that his classmates and mentors did not know how to deal with a disabled boy, since he was the only one in the campus. When his family shifted to Noida, he was admitted to APJ School, a disabled friendly institution, owned by Satya Paul, who was himself disabled. Since he was left out of most school activities, he spent his childhood years reading. This made him the most well-read boy in school. He went on to top Business Studies, Nationally, while he was in the 12th standard with 92 per cent. That saw him featured in the newspapers and changed his image in school, where he began to be recognized as a nerd, rather than one with disability.

Besides reading, his other love was cricket. 'If I cannot play cricket, I can be a commentator,' He remarked. So he requested Harsha Bhogle; the well known cricket commentator, to be his pen-pal. This was when he discovered his love for writing, which he pursues even today, as an active blogger. 'Throughout my life, I find I need to work harder, to show my motivation and desire to excel,' he reflected. Citing examples from his life, he spoke about his college days. He had decided to enroll in St. Stephen's College for pursuing an honors degree in Economics. On being asked in his entrance interview, if he would be ready to be carried up to the first floor every day, he replied with a resounding 'yes'. After the first four days of actually seeing a disabled person's motivation to attend classes, the administration decided to shift the classrooms at the ground level, changing the course of its 125 years history!

It was at Stephen's College, that he sowed the seeds of his advocacy work, which later, blossomed into the Nipman Foundation. He began actively working with fellow disabled students, to set up an 'Enabling Committee' on the campus. This committee was entrusted with installing ramps for wheel chairs, JAWS software for the visually impaired and so on. During this time, he also realized that he wanted to become an entrepreneur. His inspiration was closer home, where his father had founded a business, moving on from the family business in Mumbai. 'It all began with four family members in one single bedroom. Today, there are three factories with 300 skilled people. I realised an entrepreneur can create visible impact by creating jobs,' he elucidated. To hone his skills, during 2009-2010, he started the St. Stephen's Entrepreneurship Cell. His initiative has taken roots; growing into an incubator of student enterprises.

Unlike many, who apply for a degree under the disability quota, Nipun always opted for the general category. The specialisation chosen was the media to help him become a cricket commentator. The interviews however, in media companies, he found much to his dismay, focussed on his disability rather than his abilities. Even after seven rounds of interview, for a sports channel, he was rejected on the ground of the office toilets not being disabled friendly. 'These deep mindsets are what I have to contend with ... even now, in my journey as an entrepreneur!' On flights, he is asked whether he would be able to fly, as he is on a wheel chair. While in a pub, the bearer looks at his friends, seeking approval for his drink. When he is interviewing staff, other members hesitate to look at him, feeling uncomfortable by his presence. 'It's so funny! It's out and out hilarious! They somewhere, refuse to believe that a wheel-chaired person can be in a position of influence'.

Narrating an incident of an industrial fair that he attended, he recounts, 'The Vice-President of the Marketing division, of an automobile product did not take me seriously. Well, he lost out on a huge order!' To prevent any embarrassment, he conducts most meetings in familiar coffee shops, since the table has to be of a certain height, for his wheel chair. Furthermore, the bearers recognise him and know that Nipun sips all beverages with a straw; including his tea.

In 2012, he started the Nipman Foundation, which works on health, dignity and happiness for those with disability. The foundation works actively with government institutions, like the railways, to ensure inclusion and accessibility. For accessible elections, they sensitized officers at the election booths, to the needs of the disabled. They even conducted an accessibility audit for the Government of Maharashtra. They also help those youngsters, who are not eligible for such government support, by getting them wheel chairs. Speaking about education, they have actively helped the disabled youth, in setting up small enterprises – A tailoring or a tea shop. All initiatives are directed at making the fraternity economically independent, thereby raising their confidence. The Foundation constituted the Equal Opportunity Award in 2014, to felicitate companies which promoted employment of disabled people. His passion is however, advocacy for the cause – he speaks at tech companies, conferences expanding on the fact that it's the attitudes that disable. And sometimes, narrating tales from his own life – of four security guards blocking his way to enter Keya, a restaurant in Delhi, citing that the disabled were not permitted.

In Nipman Fastners, Nipun worked with the Tata Strategy Management group, drawing out a five year plan. The roadmap is to take the present turnover; INR 120 crores to INR 600 crores in five years. This roadmap, he expands, has helped him in making the company professional. They have hired vice-presidents for operations, business development and engineering. Further, a non-family Director was appointed for the first time. They have also decided to diversify into steering system components and signed up with a Korean organization.

'People don't really expect that a disabled person can be an entrepreneur … can be on an equal footing! It's time that their lame beliefs are challenged and they are thrown out of their comfort zone. But that's why I'm there – to prove them wrong and succeed,' said Nipun, with his ever green optimism.

MANTRAS FOR SUCCESS

1. Live in the moment. Cross the immediate hurdles, rather than worrying about the future.
2. Dream big but remain focused.
3. Disability education needs to be taught in school itself, like sex education.

Nirmal Kumar

The user-friendly auto service, from the portals of a premier management institute

'Abdul Kalam; the former President of India, has just praised my work', reads the Whatsapp message over my hand-held device, with a voice byte of the recently deceased President. The message is from Nirmal; founder of G-Auto, who succeeded in creating a new image for the auto drivers. His endeavour was to make the auto-ride friendly and secure, yet a low cost transportation experience.

Nirmal is not very tall, his physique being polio affected. He is a free-spirited person, whose energy levels and enthusiasm is envious. In his journey of setting up G-Auto, and then scaling it up vertically, he has pursued and met various dignitaries, including the then Chief Minister of Gujarat; now Prime Minister – Narendra Modi. Photographs of such moments are prominently displayed alongside his countless awards. Like the International Grand Mobility Award – Xcellon, Volvo Sustainability

Mobility Award and the iUT 2014 Award. 'You can be handsome but not harbouring the right attitude for work. For being a successful entrepreneur, physical looks are irrelevant,' he states.

Nirmal is a Bihari, who has made Gujarat; India's bed of enterprise, his home. He hails from a small village of Maharajgang, in Siwan district, from Bihar. His father was a village school teacher. Education was always a struggle. Attending primary school meant sitting on gunny bags, in a small tin-shed class room and quite often, the teachers marked their presence by their absence. Polio prevented him from both, walking and cycling to high school. 'I used to teach students at the recess time and they obliged back, by giving me a lift on their bikes!' He smiled, his grateful eyes twinkling. Hailing from an agricultural family, Nirmal had often brooded about his future. As destiny had planned, he won the competitive ICAR scholarship and came to the BR Ranga Institute; Hyderabad for his B.Sc in agriculture. The campus was green and beautiful. Though boys like him, with rural backgrounds were bright; students with convent and city backgrounds answered the questions in class. Their edge was their spoken English skills. Nirmal, hence, went on to form a club; Phoenix, where rural youth could meet and interact, helping each other to improve their grip on English. Soon, these so-called country bumpkins were confident of themselves, sweeping trophies in college debates. 'It was such a learning. Changes do happen with some effort ... so never feel defeated,' he mused. This is one lesson that he imbibes in present day business too. Like others from his home-town Bihar, he too, after graduation, began preparing for his IAS. That is when he learnt about the Common Aptitude

Test or CAT. All that he knew about CAT was that it was a magic wand, which could help a person earn an astronomical figure of INR forty-five lakhs. As he cleared the same, he secured a seat for himself in IIM Ahmedabad. Once in his second year, he realized that earning in lakhs was too small a dream. He was meant for bigger things.

The idea to set up G-Auto happened over a trivial incident. He and his friends took an auto from the IIM campus to a restaurant, for dinner. Though the auto driver charged INR twenty-five for one way, he charged INR forty-five for travelling the same distance, back to the campus. However, the driver could not give a rational explanation for this difference in fare. This disturbed Nirmal, who then decided to embark upon a longer journey. He wanted to build India's first sustainable, friendly and reliable auto service. 'Why cannot the auto ride be a delightful and safe experience, with no haggling?' He quizzed in rhetoric. To understand the psyche of the auto drivers, he spent his evenings and weekends interacting with them. He asked them, that if he were to give them incentives like – medical insurance and helped them stock newspapers and magazines in their vehicles, would they be courteous? Ten auto drivers thought this made sense. This prompted him to borrow money and pay the insurance premium. Subsequently, G-Auto was born.

Soon, the first hundred drivers called in. The dilemma was how to finance their insurance, since he already had an educational loan. So he prepared an intensive and exhaustive power-point presentation, working on a borrowed laptop. This was then offered to companies as branding slots. Almost immediately, Reliance came on board. He then, used this advertising money to bring 100 more vehicles under the G-Auto fold. Thereafter, he wrote to the Chief Minister, asking for 15 minutes to present his ideas. While presenting them, he requested Narendra Modi to inaugurate the project of 1000 autos in his constituency; Maninagar. With such a concrete foundation and road-map, there was no looking back. Of course, like all start-ups, there were challenges, like the Auto union, which needed to be handled in a pragmatic manner.

Today 15,000 G-Autos ply in Ahmedabad, Gandhinagar, Vadodara, Rajkot and Surat. With scale, Nirmal incorporated the use of technology, the concept of service and segmented the trainings. All autos carry water, newspaper, magazines, mobile chargers and a number where-in the customers can call, for lodging any complaints. The fares are transparently displayed and all customers are given a receipt. 'I had asked the auto drivers about terming them pilots. They unanimously agreed, citing that it would bring them dignity and respectability'. The auto drivers, now called pilots, were given training in English, Hindi alongside basic customer management skills. The add-ons include G-Auto for tourism; a partnership with the Ahmedabad Municipal Corporation. Drivers are given a tour of the heritage city and lessons in history with different packages. Media gave considerable coverage where the auto drivers were termed as 'The city's new brand ambassadors'. More recently, a new service added at the Ahmedabad airport is the G-Auto Airport expressway service. 'My aim is to keep all the stakeholders happy. Give 3 S's (Suraksha, Samridhhi and Samman) – security, prosperity and dignity to the much neglected auto driver. And for the commuter, solve the RATS problem – Refusal, Accessibility, Transparency and Safety,' he remarked proudly.

Auto drivers carry smart phones, which can help track the vehicle. A 24x7 call centre receives all enquiries, calls and patiently handles the complaints. Safety being the focal point is ensured for women and children, even for those who work the graveyard shifts. In fact, with rape incidents in Delhi and safety becoming a serious concern, G-Auto has spread its wheels to the Capital. 'The revenue model is simple,' he elucidated. For every ride, INR fifteen is the service charge. Customers do not mind paying, as they get flawless service and are saved from arguing over the fares.

The multinational Uber, is launching Uber Auto, based on the G-Auto model. This has forced Nirmal to don his thinking cap. 'One can't feel threatened by the power of a multinational. It's time I expand. This has been my baby … who can ride over a pioneer?' He pauses ere he continues, 'To be candid, I never really realised the power of my model. When I see that multinationals are adopting it … I want to take the enterprise to newer heights, with a first mover advantage!' He has made presentations to various venture capitalists. His vision is to scale up to hundred cities in the next five years. He is not however, resting on the laurels of his auto venture, for he feels that everyone must give back to the society. Nirmal Foundation connects unemployed youths to jobs. As we step out of his office together, he sheds light on his next meeting, aimed at networking with yet another powerful CEO, to oil the wheels of his auto dreams.

MANTRAS FOR SUCCESS

1. Disability is a state of mind. It must never deter you from fulfilling your dreams.
2. Keep the fire in the belly going. Physical perfection is not everything.
3. Be mentally strong. Work should be your worship.

Raghu Shenoy

A serial software entrepreneur on a wheel chair.

'The only difference between my engineers and me, is that they sit on wooden chairs, while I use a wheel-chair!' Our conversation begins with this unusual perspective on disability. Raghu Shenoy is the founder of the Bangalore based 'Bit By Bit Computer Services'; a reputed software firm that focuses on product development for select International clients. From a one man office, Raghu has grown phenomenally. His company is now worth half a million dollars. Apart from success, name and fame, he even found love in his work-place. He has married Usha; an engineer, who once worked as a part of his team. A balanced family person, he drives to his office in Bande; Nallasandra in his sleek modified BMW and is back home by 6 PM. Once home, he play-acts dinosaur stories and plays interactive science games with his five year old daughter.

What strikes me about Raghu is his attitude towards disability. As Raghu fixes me a cappuccino in his open kitchen, we begin a delightful conversation, wherein, I present a contrarian view. Later Raghu, Usha and I dig into a delicious Thai salad with a spicy pizza. The word 'handicap,' he explains, 'comes from beggars who used their caps to get alms'. As he speaks, I learn that 'disabled' and 'handicapped' were used synonymously, at one point of time. He believes that once the 'subsidy' or 'special privileges' mentality sets in, people really get handicapped. For example, 'Yes, I spend on a wheel-chair, but my shoes last a lifetime'. Any situation can be looked at positively. All challenges, he believes, lie in one's head. His 'think positive' attitude stems from his mother's words, which he regularly quotes – 'There is only one answer to "How are you" and it is "Fine, Thank you!"'

He was confined to a wheel chair while he was completing his Masters degree at the Indian Institute of Technology; Madras. He recounts, 'It happened all of a sudden … so utterly unexpected!' Suffering from high fever, he was riding a scooter, enroute to his uncle's place nearby, for lunch. Suddenly, he felt the scooter was not stopping at the red light. 'I thought the brakes had malfunctioned … little did I know that my life had altered its course!' It was not the brake, but his legs. He had lost out on motor functioning. By the end of the day, he was taken to the hospital, bundled onto a stretcher. The diagnosis was rather unclear. The medical experts could not conclude whether it was a virus or bacterial infection of the spine. They were of the opinion that diseases related to the brain were curable, but the spinal damage was irreversible. After eight months of shuttling in and out of the hospital, he recovered to a stage where he could read and write. Once out of the hospital, he registered a company. 'People ask me what is better – being born disabled or becoming disabled. Having a L1 spine injury or C1? I don't think it's any different. The problem arises when you have a choice. Most disabled people do not have that. When I went on a wheel chair, I had two choices – To sit in a corner and weep or simply continue. Was there a choice?' His tone is curt but his eyes exude warmth.

'Bit By Bit' operated out of a house in Bangalore, with one engineer. Most of the work was for small scale industries in Bangalore itself. It involved helping them in their transition from program logic control to PC control, since computers were still priced at just under a lakh in the 1990's. Their first big client was 'Baumhart' and retains the same standing till date. In 1997, John Hart; a partner, having heard of the Silicon Valley of India, decided to come to Bangalore, to tie up with a local company. He visited the IT giants and signed up with one of them. On his way to the airport, he stopped over at Bit By Bit and gave them a small contract. The giant company could not deliver even after one year and Bit By Bit got the entire pie to itself. The task assigned was to develop a product for a hospital. Bit By Bit began making a tool for the seamless management of the temporary staff of the hospital. That contract changed the course of history for Raghu.

Today, thirty-two engineers work on the product, incorporating changes and redesigning it as required. Meanwhile, the company has changed hands and is now a part of 'Allocate Software'; an organization hosting 3,000 plus knowledge workers. However, Raghu remains with the product, even though the product ownership is no longer with him. 'It is like a successful doctor's practice. A customer came to us offering half a million dollars. But that would have left me with no time for my family. So I made a conscious choice!' He elaborates, harping on the importance of being a family man. 'Most people do not define what they want from life. As if, they are not clear about their life goals. Thankfully, I am sorted. All I want is … to buy books without glancing at its price tag and affording one holiday every year, without worrying about the cost!'

Looking back, much of his philosophy is influenced by a home where education was valued. For his third birthday, he was given the entire '*Encyclopaedia Britannica*'. 'I'm sure my father must have slogged himself to buy that for me'. His grandfather was a mathematics teacher in a village. Some of the stories that he narrated are still held closely by Raghu. For instance, being reprimanded for taking a jackfruit from the school compound.

Raghu, a mathematics wizard is also a fantastic accountant. Even in the earlier days, when many women were forbidden from pursuing university studies, his mother and her sisters were all highly educated. This academic influence made young Raghu opt for engineering, followed by his Masters degree from IIT Madras.

Even after establishing a successful company, Raghu's entrepreneurial streak continues unabated. He with two of his friends is forming a new company. 'Think 7' – focussing on product development for the automobile industry. One of the partners has been making parts for the automobile industry, as an ancillary for the last sixteen years. The other partner has marketing experience in SAP sales. Raghu remains the software expert. The new company has been set up with low costs, not wanting to avail of outside funding. The Alpha testing was done at one partner's site and the office remains at the Bit By Bit address. The automobile product focuses on quality and reducing rejection. So the market, he is hopeful, shall be bright even if the industry is down presently.

Alongside work, a friend, Dr. Ali Khwaja, thought Raghu would be good at counselling and motivating others confined to wheel-chairs. 'I met this girl ... she wanted to kill herself! I explained her that life is the same ... for those with and without the wheel-chair. The sun still shines on every one, the grass is green under the feet, regardless of their disability! What is a wheel-chair? It is just a tool. Just like spectacles. If someone wears spectacles, to adjust their vision, do we call them disabled?' His views are refreshing and soothing. He is clear that a wheel-chair cannot define him. And this spirit has let Raghu wander alone, in far off places, from North Arctic to Zanzibar. While India does not have accessible cities, his experience is that Indians are helpful.

Raghu frequently quotes his paraplegic friend, Robert Kohli. The latter chose to leave Switzerland and settle in Bangalore. 'You know what Kohli said ... That in Zurich, businesses are accessible, but here in India, the people are!' He goes on to cite an incident. Just after his accident, he accompanied his cousin to a movie theatre. After he had bought the tickets, he was left wondering how to navigate his wheel chair up the stairs, as there was no elevator. It was then, that four friends, who were but on-lookers lifted the wheel-chair and escorted him till the theatre. After the movie, he was moved to tears, upon seeing the same four boys, who stated, 'We took you in ... so obviously, we have to get you out!'

In his spare time, he hopes to mentor young minds, to help

them think creatively, spin stories and to believe that nothing is impossible!

MANTRAS FOR SUCCESS

1. Think positive.
2. Be clear about your goals.

Sabriye Tenberken

She runs a centre for global change-makers, despite being blind!

An hour's drive from Trivandrum, one can be at Kanthari; a campus of verdant greenery. Once at the sprawling campus, one can witness scores of students walking around, engrossed in deep discussion. As I walk till the lake, adjacent to the property, my eyes fall on Sabriye. I am here to meet her and I see her returning from her daily swim regime.

Sabriye defies every stereotype of a blind person. She has gone on horseback in Tibet to set-up a school for the blind, and has now, set up a unique centre for the socially disadvantaged people, including those with disability. These people are her agents of change. Her work stems from a philosophy, that there is beauty in blindness, rendering the blind with a distinct advantage that they can tap into. She has won the coveted Mother Teresa Award, Time Magazine's Asia's Hero Award and was also nominated for the Nobel Prize in 2005.

Her mission is rather simple – she yearns to kantharize the world. Elucidating her mission, she explains, 'Kanthari is the name of a chilli plant that grows wild in the backyard, in this part of India. It has a fiery taste that makes you sit up and take notice when you bite into it ... yet, it has medicinal properties. Our criteria for registration here is not a formal degree, but every one of them, should have had overcome some adversity ... or should be marginalised in some manner. We want our students to make a difference akin to a Kanthari'. I gape at her confidence.

She, along with her sighted partner; Paul Kronenberg, decided to set up an institute which would help youth from the marginalised communities, to become a springboard for change. They chose India; they chose Trivandrum. They felt India was central in the world map; it was developing and yet, there was tremendous scope for change. 'We were delighted to spot this three and a half acre of greenery with its own lake! We would hear the birds whistling and the swish of the fish, as it jumped,' she squealed in delight.

Her vision was clear since the inception. She wanted to set up a global dream factory, where the marginalised and the disabled could carry out their dreams and become social visionaries. Initially, when they shared their ideas about the institute, there was apparent disbelief. How can the institute have no professors, no academics and the students be taken on without any formal degrees? Why cannot it be another IIM? 'We wanted to shift the focus from social entrepreneurs to social change-makers, for the former has a business color to it. After all, Gandhi and Mandela did not do business. So like the Kanthari, which has various hues, one of the colours can be business!' The curriculum was planned as a journey with five acts, encompassing experiential learning. For example, students go through a virtual world, where they have every kind of experience. Learning takes place by making mistakes. The entire focus is on practical skills – Public speaking, Business modelling, Dealing with the Government, Encountering the media and Raising funds. By the end of the course, each Kanthari is connected to potential donor agencies. This means that by the time the student leaves, each is well equipped to roll out a project in the real world, in his home country.

Out of the 117 young men and women who participated in the course, one runs a mobile library for prisoners in Thailand while another blind student, indulges in bee-keeping in Uganda, selling its honey to Italy. Sabriye speaks of Beatriz Quispe, a blind woman from Peru, who made the long journey to India via North America. She came boldly, unescorted by train from Mumbai. She has since started a mobile blind school, back in the Andes Mountains.

The seed of this work in Kanthari was sown in 'Braille without Borders'; the organisation Sabriye and Paul set up in Tibet. The school was a dream house for the blind children. There they could learn mobility and fuel their dreams of becoming a scientist or a micro entrepreneur. In Kanthari, the canvas was stretched to include the marginalised with the disabled, though the core idea remained unaltered.

Sabriye was born in Koln; Germany, with retinal pigmentosis. In this disease, the vision fades gradually. By the time she was all of fourteen years, she was completely blind.

Deciding to leave her home country, apprehensive about their nagging ways, she relocated to Tibet. 'The right to take risk and responsibility is always equal between those with sight and those blind!' Remarked Sabriye, who always has had a spark for adventure. Her first experience of working was with Red Cross, who hesitated to send her to the field. So, she decided to set up something of her own.

She rode on horseback while in Tibet, trying to understand the plight of the blind children. Tibet, steeped in spirituality had always appealed to her. She had taught herself Tibetian Braille, Mandarin and Chinese. As I probed about her riding a horse, she replied, 'Well a horse is better than a car. Since there is no glass window between you and the people ... Also, the horse will not fall into a ravine!'

In Tibet, there are 33,000 blind, in a population of 2.62 million. The figures are alarming because of the strong Ultra Violet radiation. Tibetians believe in the law of karma and that blindness is a punishment for the wrongs committed in the past life. She discovered children kept in dark rooms, tied to a bed and therefore, could not walk. That helped her find her purpose, as she began a school with eight rescued blind children. Paul Kronenberg, who worked with the Red Cross, soon joined her. Thus, 'Braille without Borders' was born. The children are taught mobility training to be independent; basic school education and skills like weaving, vending, massaging to help them be economically independent. Today, some of the children are integrated into regular schools; others have started successful micro enterprises like vending butter tea; massage parlours and so on. Some enterprises like cheese making, printing press and animal husbandry begun by the duo, are now run by the community. In the beginning, no one believed that a blind woman was capable of running a project. This led to scarce funding. Sales from Sabriyes book, which was translated into twelve languages from German, helped in running 'Braille without Borders'. For this work, Sabriye and Paul were awarded the Knights medal from the Queen of Netherlands. The Ambassador made a special trip to Lhasa to give away this prestigious award to the deserving duo.

Sabriye laments about the condition of the blind in India. 'They are over-protected and do not use their abilities. Everyone feels that the blind are a problem, which needs to be solved or an imperfection to be corrected. But the sighted cannot think like the blind. So the sighted need to step back and give the blind a platform to empower themselves,' she sighs. 'Since people with disability in India think they have a handicap, they themselves ask for reservation. And in these reservation jobs, they are not active. Many just get salary and sit. It is sad and demeaning and adds fuel to the common perception that the disabled are not capable of hard work'.

Recounting a school visit, where she asked blind kids to describe the beauty of blindness, she was taken aback. There was a complete silence in the class, for they had heard such a thing for the first time. No one had uttered these words before. Finally, one young boy piped up, saying he can read under his blanket in the night, without his mother knowing and no one else can do this. Another joined in and shared that he remembers numbers better than his siblings. 'This positive spirit is an indicator that every child with disability is capable! They can do anything that they set their heart upon. This message needs to be instilled in the schools!'

As I shake hands to leave, mesmerised by this remarkable woman, Sabriye says, 'Remember, if I was not blind, I never could have had set up Kanthari. And here, we are not interested in candles that flicker … We want to build fires! Fires that burn for a long time! That will usher in a global change'.

MANTRAS FOR SUCCESS

1. Value your limitations and train your other senses.
2. Remember there is beauty in disability.
3. Take risks, be adventurous and above all … dream.

Sanjay Dang

He has travel details at his fingertips, though he cannot see!

'Good afternoon, Ramesh ji'

'Singapore Airlines; Mumbai – London on Wednesday? The time is 0130'

'Swissair; Mumbai-Frankfurt, it's 0215'

'London, England; Travelworld. com – do look at our website'

Both – the fixed-line and the hand-held ring incessantly. There are calls soliciting detailed information on complicated routes, tight schedules, new visa regulations and various other queries. Sanjay churns out information; his eyes closed. He doesn't require a guidebook or even a computer.

Sanjay is in his forties and can be aptly classified as a highly successful travel entrepreneur. Today, *Le Travel World*, his company, is valued at INR ninety crores, offering customers a wide range of services. The services encompass travel itineraries, insurance, hotel packages and bespoke tours. He has offices in Noida and Connaught Place. Last night, he returned from a travel conference in Muscat and is back in his office today morning, on the dot of nine. His office set-up comprises of ten team members but for the clients, Sanjay remains the preferred contact point.

His mother was worried about little Sanjay's frequent falls and the squint in one of his eyes. After several rounds of tests at the Army Hospital, he was diagnosed with high myopia. He lost vision in one eye by the age of seven. He attended the Army School in New Delhi and the Kendra Vidyalaya in Bareilly and Dehradun. Active in dramatics, he even contributed regularly to the school magazine. But even slight movements and jerks meant that his retina would be displaced. Thereafter, it had to be inserted back, by cryopexy and other surgical devices, once or twice a year. The doctors felt this intrusive surgery was happening too often. The other eye was so fragile, that after completing his class X from the Army school, he opted for distance education. 'Medicine was not so advanced way back in 1974,' he sighed. Reading could only be done by keeping the object at close proximity to his eyes.

He also had macular degeneration, which resulted in loss of vision from the centre of his visual field. By the age of twenty-five, he was blind. 'This meant that my education was not what a regular classroom offered. For hours, I listened to BBC, Deutsche Welle and CNN, absorbing the information like a sponge,' he stated. Little did he dream, that one day this knowledge of the customs, culture and communication styles of the world would help him become a first class travel agent!

His mother, sister and brother moved to Delhi when his father had a non-family posting in Siliguri; West Bengal. This helped him access the best of retinal specialists like Dr. Patnaik, as his other eye was also weakening due to Retinitis Pigmentosa.

As he was reading the paper one day, he chanced upon a vacancy in a travel house. The job was in his neighbourhood; Rajouri Garden. It asked for work experience which he did not have. Nevertheless, the fighter in him applied and even got the post. The Manager of the GSA of Pan Am was pleasantly taken aback at his wealth of knowledge about global travel. 'I told him about the new FRA rules. About the proposed company takeovers like Kuoni taking over Sita,' Sanjay recounted with a wide grin. Initially, his role was to answer calls and pass the information on, onto others. However, in less than a month, he had managed to surpass the expectation of his superiors and was elevated onto a different level. Now, he was entrusted with pre and post service for the clients directly. This is how his journey began.

When the family moved to their own house in Noida, Sanjay decided it was time to set up his own travel agency. 'Those were the challenging days. But then, they were good fun! I operated with one chair, a table and a phone. I had an assistant, who rode a scooter and dropped cheques alongside picking up air tickets. Well, I had borrowed some funds from my father. But then, they were limited … so, I had to resort to unusual advertising in a bid to be seen!' The adverts screamed, 'Lowest airfares – Delhi to Dubai'. Like a lot of start-ups, he used free space newspapers like Noida Times. 'I had to make people call me! That was the only challenge. Once a call came … I knew what was required to close the deal'.

In those days, travel agents had only one or two fixed-lines, which too, were constantly busy. A secretary of the chairman of a Noida based company was rather frustrated as she could not reach out to her regular travel agent. Retrieving Sanjay's number from the Noida Times newspaper, she enquired about the Swissair first class fares from Mumbai to London. Not only did he furnish the details, but also told her that since her boss was in Delhi, he could try getting the Thai first class flight, direct from Delhi. In the evening, a limousine arrived at their house and the gentlemen asked for Sanjay. The industrialist was the late Mr. Vachani of the largest electronic conglomerate; Weston Electronics. He could not believe that a young man with a disability, sitting in the garage, was the travel agent. 'This was my first 'First Class' ticket and then, there was no looking back,' smiled Sanjay. So impressed was Mr. Vachani with his services, that he recommended Sanjay to his family and friends in Hong Kong and other cities alike.

Those days there was no internet. Anyone travelling abroad relied on borrowed information. For instance, a student would call for a ticket to London, when his actual destination was Cardiff. He had obviously got the information that there were no flights to Cardiff. Sanjay would offer a slightly more expensive ticket, but a direct one. 'You see, there was a difference between me and the other agents. The latter were mere order takers'. Sanjay indulged in asking questions, wanting a clearer picture of the clients' requirements. His unique selling proposition was his custom-designed itineraries at a value-for-money rate.

Online bookings have altered the very outlook of the travel industry and these new companies have large advertising budgets. 'We continue to have the same customers. We offer unparalleled services. I am available even at eleven pm. All this leads to loyalty. It is this quality of service that ensures Le Travel World does well ... even in a competitive environment.

I am proud of the fact, that I do not need a sales and marketing team. Neither do I require advertising!' He reflects confidently.

The mainstay is corporate travel, but the agency handles insurance and transportation too — the entire gamut of services required by a traveller. He sells travel overseas and also caters to the outbound customers. The office in Connaught Place is managed by his brother; a dentist. 'My brother preferred this business over dentistry. Why wait for patients when you have customers waiting in this business'. His father, a Brigadier, took early retirement and helps them oversee the finances.

Intrigued, I ask, 'Do people come to you ... just out of kindness?' He immediately retorts, 'My customers feel good and come because of the services I give. With poor service, business cannot be sustained,' he states. George of Eyeway is a regular client. He had called upon Sanjay, several years back, when his wife was travelling to London. He offered a fare via Korea which suited his budget. 'It was only when George came to fetch the ticket that he learnt about my blindness!' I quiz him again, 'How did you cope with the challenges?' Quick to reply, he remarked, 'I was lucky! If you realize, blindness did not happen suddenly to me. I had enough time to prepare myself mentally. This helped me to reflect ... to think out-of-the box'.

He has evolved skills, he explains, which are normal for a person with visual impairment, but they come as a real surprise to the others. 'It is a fact ... that you will have enhanced memory retention and recall. Other faculties become stronger when your visual functions are limited or nonexistent. I'm better with information. Phone numbers and addresses come naturally to me. Also, I can recognize voices better than others'.

Voice recorders and other gadgets have definitely helped him along the way. He relies on technology and is well-versed with the latest developments, which serve as aids to the visually impaired. 'It is prudent to keep checking at frequent intervals, if these products have improvised versions. Technology, like life, is always in a flux!' He states philosophically.

MANTRAS FOR SUCCESS

1. Think of your strengths and concentrate on them.
2. Think about what you can do and achieve.
3. Be happy with what you have. Being content is all that matters.

Shivani Gupta

Mainstreaming accessibility is her passion!

Shivani is a bundle of energy. As I bid her adieu, I turn around to see her double bolting her Vasant Kunj flat door. As I saunter out, braving the Delhi heat, I am compelled to admit that life indeed, is stranger than fiction. For how else can one justify an overnight accident, disabling a twenty-two year old for life? From a care-free, fashionable hotelier to a tetraplegic, life has not been a bed of roses for Shivani. But then, life seldom comes without harsh learnings! One car accident followed another. Twenty years after the first one transpired, she lost her husband; Vikas. They were very much in love and had recently tied the knot.

I wondered about her indomitable spirit! Where did she get the strength from? To pick up the pieces and become a whole again? To pursue her dream of an accessible India for the disabled community at large? To then, becoming a social entrepreneur and setting up 'Access Ability', which gives professional services to organisations who want to be access friendly.

At twenty-two, she worked as a guest-relations officer at Hotel Maurya Sheraton. Cinderella hour, as she was dropping her friends off, the chauffeur suddenly braked, so as to avoid hitting a stray animal. The jolt was tremendous. She flew out of the car and came crashing onto the ground. Her spine was injured beyond repair. After six months of treatment in various hospitals, she reconciled to the fact that she would never walk again.

Of course, the tears would not stop. But bit by bit, steadfastly, she began getting a grip on herself. The inspiration came from her grandparents, as she lived with them in Faridabad. Under their selfless support, she began gaining control over some muscles, moving around in a wheel-chair. 'I was transported to my childhood. Then, it was about walking, jumping and running. Now, it was about taking small steps in the wheel-chair. Being positive always helps!' She smiled briefly. It was the society pressure which ailed her though. Once at a temple, someone gave her a coin. And why? She was neatly dressed! It struck her then, that despite being clad in neat clothes, the lady had mistaken her for a beggar, just because she was disabled. Hence, began her quest to stand up for the disabled society, looking beyond her own limitations and tapping into her abilities instead.

Shivani had enrolled for a peer counselling course in the United Kingdom. She observed, that there all the buildings were accessible, rendering her freedom to shop and to socialise. Back home, instead of counselling the wealthy, in a hospitality career, she chose to encourage others like her. So for six years, she counselled the disabled at the Institute of Spinal Injuries. The defining point of her life was a course in non-handicapping environment in Bangkok, with Vikas, a fellow occupational therapist, who she later married and lost.

This area of inclusive physical environments interested both of them. Together, they thought about the possibilities in India. While Vikas and she went separate ways; he to the United Kingdom for work and she to Delhi, the realization of the gnawing accessibility gap knocked at their minds. Deciding to widen her knowledge, she went ahead with a degree course in architecture, at the Rai University. 'I had the double handicap of age and disability but my determination overcame them,' she said in a matter-of fact tone.

When an opportunity arose to do a Masters in Inclusive Environment, at the University of Reading (United Kingdom), she had to raise substantial funds. 'When you feel something is of significance, pursue it! In my case, the expenses are for two. I am always with my caregiver,' she highlighted. She got a loan from the National Handicap Finance Development Corporation, a Tata scholarship and sponsorship from Sminu Jindal Trust. Alongside, she also received INR 1.50 lacs from the Neerja Bhanot Award. All of these, coupled together, helped her to fly out to pursue her studies.

In India, disability is by default, a charity issue. That the disabled are poor and require subsidies is the dominant policy makers' attitude. The reality though, is inaccessibility. It does not allow the disabled to participate in regular activities such as education, employment, entertainment and so on. To cite, there is no suitable infrastructure, access to information and communication, access to the public transportation system and general public awareness. As a result, the disabled remain with low literacy and employment levels; pushing the wheel of the vicious cycle of poverty. To make a break-through, Access Ability was formed by Shivani and Vikas along with Sachin Varma in 2006. Sachin had just returned with a Masters degree in Information Technology from Australia. The vision was to mainstream disability, as access was a major spoke in the wheel for the disabled to lead independent lives. From the beginning, they were clear that this was a social enterprise, where the clients had to pay for the services. The services ranged from access audit and appraisal to sensitivity workshops for employees and employability. 'We were professionals with degrees and experience, but were apprehensive whether the Indian customers would pay!' She recounted. Work began trickling in slowly, but in a steady pace. They had their hands full with a feasibility study for the forty-two acre campus of National Institute of Visually Handicapped in Dehradun; ITC for its hotel chain, Indian School of Business for its new campus in Hyderabad, University of Hyderabad for its sprawling Gachibowli campus and Deutsche Bank, to name a few.

If setting up Access Ability was a dream come true, there was another in the waiting. Vikas's parents, who were not happy with his marriage decision, finally relented. 'Obviously I was ecstatic. That they had agreed was phenomenal news. The marriage was in April ... But dark clouds lurked. Four months later, on the way to Manali, a car accident killed Vikas

and his father. It was traumatic; leaving me to question God
and wonder why I had to suffer. It took me a lot of time to
resign to the reality … but yes, life does move on!'

'The Government should lead this accessibility initiative,'
she reflects. 'Mere rules and policies are not enough … these
need implementation. The challenges still exist. Procurements
are not accessible'. All flagships programs have quotas for the
disabled but are not based on any universal design principle.
Tenders for audit go to the lowest bidder in government projects
and it results in a vicious cycle, where infrastructure still
remains inaccessible. However, one can see a slow, methodical
change in the metros. Though India, it lies in its villages.
Even the tier-two towns, have accessibility issues resulting in
disabled children being kept at home. '… And then, then we
complain about the poor literacy levels of the disabled. This
is so hypocritical!'

The biggest challenge for her, has been rebuilding her life
without Vikas. Writing the book; 'No Looking Back' over a
period of three years was a cathartic process. It has helped her
re-evaluate her life and look ahead.

She is also pursuing her PhD, which embeds human rights
theory and community support services for the poor. 'I have
clarity of goal and the determination to achieve it … without
disability ruling my life! When I did my architecture degree
I was thirty-four. Now at forty-four, with no research skills, I
am working on a PhD. It's simple: I want to do it and will do
it!' She states emphatically, as she throws behind her two life
changing accidents and wheels into a new life, of creating a
better world for others like her.

MANTRAS FOR SUCCESS

1. Have clear and defined goals and the determination to achieve.
2. Do not let disability rule your life.
3. Belief in yourself and never lose hope.

Siddartha Sharma

He is visually impaired and runs a Public Relations firm

How does Siddartha visualise campaigns without seeing the product, its contours and colours? How does he convince clients in a competitive market? 'No customer has ever asked me, as to how I do this work ... though I am blind,' he grins. He has a modest client base; the loyalists. Lotus cosmetics has stayed with him since a decade. His advertising plans have resulted in their meteoric rise, from INR 35 to INR 350 crores. Siddartha is the founder-owner of 'Foundations PR'; an agency which focuses on promoting up-market luxury goods and life style products.

Siddarth was twenty-five, a handsome young man, in love with life. He was working with an export house and was to get married to his long term girl-friend, in the next 15 days. However, his world came to a crashing halt with a motorcycle accident, which severed his optic nerve and left him without sight. His family moved from one hospital to another, seeking advice for over a year. Finally, a Russian eye surgeon, the best in those days, operated his eyes. 'Somehow, I had already embraced blindness. I knew it was tough, a long haul and no light at the end of the tunnel!' The operation was not successful. The marriage broke when the girl succumbed to her family pressure. In this turbulent phase, what kept him going was his inner strength and a will to live on, with a smile! It was this positive spirit that made his friends include him in their parties.

To understand the world of the blind, he spent time with the Blind Relief Association. The advice given by LK Advani from the association, has provided him strength in his weakest moments, 'Remember,' said Advani, 'There are only two things you cannot do – be a pilot or drive!' He enrolled himself in a three month course of home management and mobility with the National Institute of Visually Impaired in Dehradun, to see how the other blind were surviving. Most students were children or adults born blind. Also, most were not English savvy. 'I realised two big advantages I had – I spoke English and more importantly, I had sight for twenty-four years. Others had no power of visualisation … which meant they could not comprehend what a blue sky meant. So I came back feeling far more fortunate than the others!' He resonated.

He rejoined the garment factory but realized that it was not his future calling, as he could not contribute meaningfully to printing or textile fabrication. He did odd jobs like helping a jewellery designer export her work. But all along, he felt, that that too, was not his core competence. A sense of restlessness overcame him. He pondered deeply about which work would suit his new capabilities and excite him.

A chance meeting with George Abraham of Score Foundation got him involved in the organisation committee, for the first World Cup Cricket tournament for the blind. The job given to him was public relations. On one hand, he had to reach out to 150 school principals, so that the students came to watch the matches; to cheer the blind sportsmen! On the other hand, the work involved liaising closely with Connexions; the Dalmia Public Relations agency, which had won the contract for handling the World Blind Cup. He found that he could contribute actively in all spheres – from interacting with the team, planning press conferences, doing media rounds and other allied activities. A visually impaired person doing PR for World Blind Cricket also made a deep impression on the media and got them listening. The event went off well, with a media blitzkrieg. This experience left him enriched and he realised his love for public relations. Meanwhile, Connexions, who had watched him in action during the cricket event, offered him a job. He joined as an executive in 1999, to help develop new business. In six months, he was heading operations and new business sections. Two Tata accounts, brands like Numero Uno, Red Tape and Carrier were the new businesses he got for the agency. 'I had found my calling!' He gushed. After three and a half years, he quit his job, wanting to garner experience with a multinational agency. He circulated his resume to the then top fifteen agencies, without stating his visual impairment. He got immediate interview calls from them, for his pedigree was right – Delhi Public School, experience of getting new accounts and handling credible events. 'My blindness shocked

them! They all said the same thing – "You are good but" …
The "but" was "can you make presentations? How will you
handle the situations?" They were all apprehensive!'

His friend Sajal Ghosh, who had an advertising agency
called Foundations, suggested a partnership to open a PR
agency. 'You see, I did not come from a business family. My
mother had a great job while my grandfather was a barrister. I
became an entrepreneur in September 2002 with no business
backbone … but I had requisite courage to succeed'. While
policy decisions were taken jointly, all operational issues were
handled independently by Siddartha. Their first client was
the Danish loudspeaker brand; Jamo. His former employer,
Connexions, closed down and many of their clients like Red
Tape, shifted to Foundations PR. The biggest break came two
months later, when Foundations PR bagged the World Blind
Cricket Cup account. The rationale was – That a visually
impaired persons' passion for this event would be the highest. It
was a two person agency, but passion overcame the challenges,
rendering a lifetime opportunity.

Siddartha realised he had an inherent liking for lifestyle;
be it clothing, beauty, footwear, theatre, painting or food. His
knowledge was good in these subjects, as the family subscribed
to magazines like Vogue, Harpers Bazaar amidst others. They
also discussed wine and champagne over meals. So, pubs and
fashion shows were an integral part of his life. A focus on these
brands was something he really enjoyed. Keeping this in mind,
Foundations PR created its niche of handling lifestyle brands,
in a market where a nascent market for luxury brands was
on the rise. They got the accounts of three luxury watches,

looking for people to position them in the fastest growing Indian market. These were brands like Harry Winston, Baume and Mercier. This positioning helped the agency, as the media houses knew who to turn to, when they wrote articles on the luxury market.

Sharma explained what PR means to him. 'PR means you are actually a marketing agency ... helping various marketing departments of the brands, position themselves. This means getting publicity in top magazines, getting their CEO's interviewed and thus, aggressively bringing them into the limelight. So, PR is a bridge between the media and the brand. While it is a marketing tool for companies, it works equally well for individuals and even NGO's'.

The PR field being competitive, I asked him about his Unique Selling Propositions. 'Passion, commitment and dedication are my mantras,' he elucidated. 'The market wants innovation but it also wants deliverables. We manage fantastic coverages; month after month, year after year'. Once with a client, he turns prudent. To the client, he is realistic – he does not build castles in the air, talks to him as if he sees the product and with trust in his skills. 'With less distractions, a sixth sense comes naturally,' He reasoned out. He has also dealt with clients in Europe, who are looking for a footprint in India. Ironically, he states, that the biggest challenge he faces, is not being blind, but attrition. Youngsters join his agency for the experience, hone their skills and move on. Today, without any family support, as a first generation entrepreneur, he is proud of his journey! 'In the eyes of the world ... I have a challenge, but then, I still win!'

MANTRAS FOR SUCCESS

1. Be sure of what you want to do. Research well and enjoy doing so!
2. Recognise that disability does exist. Do not make it your blind spot.
3. Be committed once you take a plunge. Entrepreneurship is a long haul. But you will succeed.

SECTION II

WISE LEADERS SHOW THE PATH

Every one of you can be a leader. In the face of challenges, you can be creative. Smart is tactical, wise is strategic. Wisdom is use of one's intelligence to solve larger problems with a noble purpose. When leaders begin to gain a wiser perspective, they can use their compassion to co-create a better world for all of us. And surprisingly, it is a solution which not only helps others, but helps their own organisation! In this book, you shall learn that these leaders, did not only create opportunities for people with disability, give youth respect, self esteem and opportunity but also leveraged their own business houses effectively; becoming wealthy and creating a strong brand presence. Here, we are sharing stories of leaders, who are wise to spot potential in others, helping them gain respect and opportunity, alongside building their self esteem. They see persons with disability with a different lens. Though the disabled might be challenged in some activity, they are challenging in other capabilities. The leaders see this as an opportunity to co-create a productive, successful workplace, one which has a ripple effect. And, perhaps most importantly, they see this as an opportunity to leave behind a better world!

Think for yourself while you read the stories herein. How can you transform yourself into becoming a true leader? What are the opportunities that you can offer to others? And in doing so, do you get to grow? Where does enlightened self-interest allow you to become successful while others around you fail? How can you move from smartness to wisdom and compassion to help you to do things that only you uniquely can?

Capt K.J. Brar

He hires youth with disability for his e-learning company.

When Aamir Khan's famed television show, 'Satyamev Jayate' focused on the subject of disability, of one of the company's featured was Designmate. Located in Ahmedabad, tucked away in the by-lanes of Navrangpura, the company makes 3D-animated educational material, which reaches over 30 countries globally. It has won awards ranging from the World Summit Award, the World Didac Award for e-learning and the Manthan Award for e-learning, to name a few. What is lesser known, is the fact that the hands which do the drawings and modeling, alongside rendering life to the animated characters, are those of the disabled. The soft spoken, gentle eyed Captain Kamaljeet Singh Brar, the man behind Designmate, echoes, 'I do what everyone should do. I am nothing exceptional. I hire people with 70–90 per cent disability ... for their abilities!'

As I walked in, I saw scores of these skilled young men and women, sitting on wheel-chairs and silently signing and communicating as they worked. As their monitors beeped to life, the screens came alive with 3D models of the human skeleton, the brain and so on. I watched spellbound, as Paresh Patel managed to navigate the animated figures with stubs as his fingers. A product by Designmate; 'Eureka' is a software program, which makes the learning of K to 12 curriculums of science and mathematics, for the children. It's a well formulated and conceptualized software, for its fun and popular with the children. 3D stereo images of science topics give a movie effect to the children and is supplemented by interactive virtual labs, quizzes, videos and puzzles. Further, the content can be mapped onto any country-specific curriculum with a bilingual facility of using English and a native language. Not surprisingly, it is available in multiple languages in 30 countries like China, Thailand, Turkey as well as the Middle-East. In Gujarat, for example, it is used by 300 private schools. To ensure that the less-privileged can afford the product, it is also given to low-cost schools on installments.

'My journey with disability began way back … in 1988 in Mumbai,' recounted the soft spoken Captain Kamaljeet Singh Brar. He had retired from the army owing to an injury. Leveraging the skills of his wife Ragini, he set up an animation studio in Mumbai; in Lamington Road. Ragini was a graphic artist, holding a degree from the prestigious National Institute of Design. This studio served as a pioneer in animation, rendering entire animation sequences, morphing, compositing and special effects. This is how the first animated video of the Indian entertainment industry was born. They pioneered 3D graphics for advertisements too. One day, a father brought his hearing impaired son to Brar, urging him to give the boy a job. The boy had a spark in his eyes. Spotting this, Brar agreed to train the boy, even though others felt it to be a waste of resources. The hearing impaired boy, turned out to become one of Mumbai's best animators. 'This ignited a spark and I decided to hire only youth with disability,' said Brar proudly.

The Brar's moved their operations to a small shed in Ahmedabad, in September 2001. The team strength was kept to ten, in a bid to reduce the overhead costs. The vision was to produce their own content and retain the Intellectual Property Rights of the same. In the past, they had produced quality content for Hollywood films, but their name never appeared in the credit mentions. Further, the margins were paltry, as they had to work as sub-contractors, under the larger production houses.

However, for the past decade, there has been no looking back. The staff of fifteen is now five hundred; the shed has been substituted by three floors of air-conditioned space in 'Horizon Towers' with the latest equipments. Of the five hundred staff, 60 per cent are severely disabled. The HR policy ensures seamless amalgamation of the recruits, from the very inception of their interviews. The rest of the non-disabled staff are academicians – teachers and computer professionals, who work on creating the educational content. 'So, all these beautiful and creative DVD's, which stimulate the child to enjoy learning physics, chemistry and mathematics are done by these youth,' he elucidates. Competition for them is largely branded, with brands like Pearson, Macmillan amongst others. 'The product is never sold or marketed using the disability angle. In this field, it is the quality which matters. Corporate Social Responsibility has no role to play here. In fact, some ignorant customers may think that the product is defective … because we hire the disabled. The USP of our merchandize is its quality and user friendliness'.

'Accessing youth with disability was difficult initially. We approached good NGO's, vocational rehabilitation centres and employment exchanges. Then, we had our teams scour the villages. Now the word has spread and the youth come on their own … even from different states. The candidates are screened for simple English and understanding of 6th grade science. They are trained free in technical skills, unlike other institutes which charge a couple of lacs as training fee,' remarked Varsha Gajjar; Adminstration manager. As most of the youth have rural backgrounds, English lessons are included. Remuneration begins from INR 6,000 monthly, increasing in proportion to one's skills. 'As they become financially independent, you should see their confidence,' she adds, visibly excited. Most of these young designers are the sole bread-winners of the family. Once viewed as a burden on their family, they are now supporting their family by their own earnings. If they have siblings, who are not disabled, the family equations change, with the disabled child earning more. 30 per cent of the disabled human resources are girls, and they are married to boys, mostly with disability. So, as a couple they earn approximately INR 50,000 monthly, which promises them a comfortable life. Poornima Dave Mistri, for example, educated herself to the Masters level at Gujarat University, despite her severe locomotor disability. She enjoys sports and has won awards in many categories – javelin, shot-put, discus throw and wheel chair racing. She works as a 3D animator at Designmate, and lives with her husband who is also disabled.

As they continue working with the disabled youth, team Designmate realizes that these designers are at par with the others. In fact some have specific skill-sets, which the company identifies and invests in. The youth with disability become the biggest assets of the company. Attrition, which troubles most BPO's, is virtually negligible at Designmate. The biggest challenge that the HR team faces is instilling the conviction that they are not disabled but professionals. 'Sign language has never been a challenge … everyone picks it up rather naturally here. Communication is easy!' smiles Varsha. This requires a massive change in ones attitude, which takes time. Many of young people have either been ignored or molly-coddled by their families. 'We explain to them to stay away from sympathy and empathy. It does not work as far as business goes,' elaborates Varsha. The thrust at Designmate is to work sincerely and to match deadlines.

The company has won the President's Award twice, for its HR policies of hiring the disabled youth. Brar's vision is to take his software to the remote villages in India, in a bid to improve the level of primary and secondary education. He hopes to help remove the existing digital divide, that will continue to be based on the terra firma of the abilities of the disabled.

ADVICE TO OTHERS

1. Have an open mind. Don't let your mind get blocked by societal attitudes.
2. Have patience, especially in beginning, while engaging with the hearing impaired
3. It is so simple – give them an opportunity, look after them and there will be no looking back.

Dhruv Lakra

His company delivers couriers silently.

Dhruv had been dreaming of setting up his own social enterprise. His background was impeccable. A working stint with Merrill Lynch, exposure to non-profit work alongside fund raising with Dasra and a management degree with the 'Saïd Business School'; Oxford. During a summer project, he was sitting on a bus, next to a deaf boy. The conductor kept announcing the stops; the boy looked thoroughly perplexed. It took Dhruv, little time to realize that the boy could not hear or speak – he was deaf. Promptly, he found himself writing on a piece of paper, making the task easier for the boy. As he wrote out the words, slowly in Hindi, he thought to himself – 'This is an invisible disability. One can't tell a thing just by looking at someone'. Once home, Dhruv looked up the statistics and found them to be rather alarming. India had a deaf population of 8 million, making it the highest in the world. Most of them had low literacy levels and unemployment was over fifty per cent. Dhruv stated the issue, 'Of the 1.7 billion population, six per cent have a hearing disorder. This meant 10 million of them. Of these sixty-six per cent are unemployed. This meant 6 million!' Could he set up an organisation which tapped into their hidden talent and showcased their competence?

Dhruv explained, 'I was home, when a boy delivered a courier silently. This set me thinking – why not start a courier service, run by the deaf ... as no communication is required'. He did not have a deep understanding of disability. His father was a paraplegic following a car accident. He had worked with mentally challenged children with an NGO in Jaipur. As he read and spoke to various deaf associations, he realised that the deaf also had great visual acuity which was critical for any courier business. Dhruv was clear on one issue. He wanted to remove existing mindsets which associated disability with charity. So he would set up a for-profit business. The business he set up would also prove a point, that the deaf can do what is considered tough – like courier delivery. 'Mirakle Couriers' was set up as a company in 2010, with the savings from his Skoll Fellowship. The first tranche of outside funding came from Echoing Green, where he won a grant of $60,000 in a global competition.

The beginnings were small. Two deaf boys joined, one of whom, Ganesh, is a supervisor today. Today, there are forty-four others doing the field deliveries. As the deaf are restricted from driving in India, they use public transport like trains and buses. 'Apart from keeping the operational costs low, this initiative of public transport is also aimed at being environmental friendly,' smiles Dhruv. Being relatively smaller, they consider flexibility to be their USP. It enables them to carry out the deliveries at the eleventh hour. The delivery boys, dressed in bright orange, with contrasting black cuffs and yellow caps; their name and Mirakle Couriers inscribed onto it, take a sense of pride in their uniform. They do not have badges indicating their disability, as the philosophy is, that they should carry out the delivery and leave. 'The magic of the game is you should not know. That is the ultimate trick. It is a delicate balance that you should not know, because the delivery personnel should deliver and go. But you should know that the delivery boy is deaf'.

The deaf are great at map reading, remembering roads and buildings owing to their visual prowess. One must look at them navigating the by lanes of Mumbai with unparalleled dexterity. The back office work is handled by six deaf girls, who had no exposure to a computer before. After getting trained in MS Office, they scan and process the delivery reports, mail sorting and data reporting. Both offices at Churchgate and Andheri; though colourful with the bright uniforms, are unusually silent. All planning and organization, including meetings are conducted in Indian Sign Language (ISL). Communications from the field are via text messages.

The biggest challenge which Dhruv faces is getting clients on board. They have doubts whether the deaf can deliver on time; whether they can handle critical documents like cheques; whether being deaf they are slow. Getting new customers is still a challenge. People do not readily give business to us. 'We need to change the perceptions. They cannot believe that such a radical idea is rather simple,' he sighs. The first order of delivering around twenty letters was given by the well-known choreographer; Shiamak Davar. Thermax allowed him to function from their Colaba office in the early days.

Dhruv then approached Indu Shahane; his college prinicipal; the wife of the Sheriff of Mumbai. She introduced him to the Mahindra's, who took a leap of faith in this innovative model. The next corporate house to back him was the Aditya Birla Group, which believes in philanthropy. The Birla's gave him office space and their head-office deliveries. 'Decision making patterns are changing in the corporate scenario. The senior management is wanting to accommodate changes and include progressive ideas, since it positions them better. However, it is the mid management, which is averse to changes. They raise queries about risks and expenses. Their first thoughts are more often than not, negative!' Making a consolidated effort to break mindsets, Mirakle Couriers approaches clients to entrust them with small order sizes, those of twenty letters. They ask the prospective clients not to give critical documents, but items like magazines, which are not time dependant. 'The problem is that at times, we get stuck with these small deliveries. It is then that we remind our clients, that our model is a proven one. If we find too much skepticism, we prefer letting go the client. All we want is an equal footing … Is it too much to ask for?' quizzes Dhruv. I ask, 'Is the rate competitive? Or do you charge higher?' Flashing a smile, he replies, 'While some customers feel good about receiving parcels that are stamped "Delivered, sorted and accounted by deaf adults", the feel good factor does not translate into any better price'. His current client base includes Vodafone, JSW, Godrej & Boyce amidst others.

Like any other business house, Mirakle Couriers too, faces the usual entrepreneurial challenges. The courier business, is a service industry with little investment requirement. Yet, expansion requires capital. Dhruv has additional challenges, because of the choices he made – of working with a disabled community. The deaf have low levels of literacy. Long spells of unemployment result in low self esteem. Further, the deaf community does not trust the outside world, since they have been deceived many a times. As a resultant, Mirakle Couriers have had to make additional investments, in not just training them in their delivery jobs, but building their self confidence and infusing a sense of belonging in them.

I find myself asking, 'How do you create this eco-sphere?' To which he replies promptly, 'To state candidly, it was not easy. Winning their confidence was a gradual process. What paid off was my honesty and transparency. The key was to understand their issues and sensitivities,' he smiled before continuing, 'Work policies also ensure ESI, PF and other entitlements. We do not believe in exploiting them'. The company works on a reference model wherein the existing workers refer new employees. Dhruv remarks, 'Parents have great influence on their disabled children. I would like to hire more girls … But their parents have issues. They are not keen on their disabled daughters travelling distances'.

Engrossed, I probe further, 'Has the government supported this model?' Dhruv is quick to reply, 'Government gives several awards. But I am done with bouquets and brass-plates. There should be a structured outlook … they must have a cash component to their awards'. He states emphatically while explaining that the main challenge is the funding. 'An Echoing green fellowship of $15,000, every six months has helped. Venture capitalists do not understand disability. They are truly not a great bunch … with so many misconceptions and apprehensions,' he rued.

Looking back, Dhruv admitted he has no regrets. 'It's sheer joy looking at these youngsters! It's a tremendous impact on them ... and their self confidence. Imagine many have savings account of INR 60,000!' A team member, Rinku, recently celebrated his wedding with his own earnings. Married young women put aside money carefully, to send their children to better schools, than what they could afford earlier.

In the near future, Dhruv aims at making Mirakle Couriers a Maharashtrian courier company. 'So the expansion model would be smaller offices in Nasik and Nagpur,' he elucidates, excitedly. While the pie is huge, paper deliveries are going down. As a result, Mirakle Couriers needs to plan its e-business arm. 'My USP is clear – To remain relatively small and flexible,' he sums up. Dhruv aims at chanting the supplier diversity mantra to invite more corporates to share his joy in this silent courier journey.

ADVICE TO OTHERS

1. Have a complete understanding of what you are getting into.
2. Match the skill set. Youth with disability cannot do everything in a business set up.
3. Integrating disability has to be a part of the culture and the very ethos of the organisation.

Ferdinand Rodricks

Rendering mobility to the disabled!

Tinkering cars at the Mahindra workshop, constantly peering from beneath the bonnet is Ferdinand Rodricks; the man behind Ferro Equip. He enables the disabled to be mobile on the roads. He is the CEO of the Mahindra & Mahindra car modification franchise. He uses this passion to modify cars and help people with different kinds of disabilities, to drive independently. Race car drivers with accidents; the polio affected; people born with physical handicaps – all stress on their need of being mobile. I quizzed a customer watching his Gypsy getting modified. 'People ask me why I cannot get a driver. Well, driving your own car makes you normal like others. It helps you to continue the activities like before! It's like attending parties and being social … this independence can really boost the morale!' He elucidated with a smile. This work recently won him the Mahatma Gandhi Samman Award, which was given by Baroness Verma at the House of Lords.

Ferdinand, who firmly believes the skill to help others is God's gift, began this work twenty-five years ago. Sanjay Joshi; his first client, had lost the usage of his legs in an accident and was confined to his wheel-chair. Ferdinand modified a Maruti Gypsy with handlebars and levers for the accelerator, brake and clutch plates. When Joshi changed his car to a Maruti Esteem, Ferdinand went a step further and installed an electronic hoist on top of the car, for the wheel chair. At the press of a button, the hoist would come down, allowing Joshi to hook the wheel-chair on to it effortlessly, after he got into his car. Joshi could now independently drive to his gas agency in Andheri, from his Borivali residence. 'I found I could fulfill varied requests quite easily. Seeing the phenomenal impact my work was making, on the lives of so many people, got me sucked into the system from which there was no turning back,' he said. Till date, he has helped over 2,000 people get on to the roads, rather effortlessly. And it's really soul-warming to see some of these smiling faces, mounted as wall photographs in his office.

Ferdinand's real break came in 2000. The British Council wrote to the Mahindra's, asking for help to make an accessible vehicle for the legendary physicist; Stephen Hawkins, on his visit to India. The challenge was that the task had to be completed in fifteen days flat. The Mahindra's proposed his name. In those days, the choice of vehicles was not varied. So he used a Mahindra Voyager and worked right through Christmas and New Year. 'I knew it was not just mine but the entire country's reputation at stake!' Smiled Ferdinand. He met Hawkins personally at the airport, to ensure he was comfortable in the vehicle. Hawkins was so pleased with the experience, that he got the hosts to take the car to Delhi by train and wrote a lovely note of appreciation.

Though Ferdinand has modified thousands of cars over the years, every car is equally special. 'There's a lot of emotion invested. Many of my customers are driving for the first time. It's like going on a first date … the joy and thrill of doing the impossible. They sit in the driver's seat and call their loved ones. "I am driving" … they squeal like a child!' Teaching the clients how to drive, while delivering the car, is a part of the package. The impact is complete independence. Suddenly, the non-mobile person finds he can do 'normal' everyday things – like driving his wife to Lonavala or taking the kids out for ice-cream in the night, like any other person, without being dependant on a driver. Many of his customers have the urge to travel. They brave challenges to clock 3,000 to 4,000 kilometers and then, discuss their escapades like any well-heeled traveler would.

Ferdinand has a degree in automobile engineering from India and in marine engineering from Hong Kong. His work experience varies from the engine room of a ship, to designing boat engines and training paramilitary teams to repair and maintain engines. His journey with automobiles began with the Tata Group. He could have remained like many others, just a corporate CEO. Says he, 'It was sheer passion that kept me on this path of making the disabled mobile'. There were hiccups in the beginning. His work could not stop with modifying cars. RTO approvals had to be taken, which directly translated into bureaucratic hurdles. 'Persistence always pays!' He smiled as he echoed a life mantra.

Today, his modified cars are approved by the Automotive Research Association of India (ARAI). It is noteworthy that the

RTO provides fifty per cent insurance exemption for his cars. The reason, he pointed out, 'is that I encourage my clients to do everything legally … and not get carried away by emotions. Road etiquette is paramount for safety. For any modification, I strictly adhere to the medical recommendations!' All his clients have to get a driving fitness certificate (For example, in Mumbai at Haji Ali), where they test their reflexes. The certificate is an indispensable clinical indicator. For instance, if the report says that the hands are the problematic zone, he simply automates that section. 'Safety and legislation are the prime concerns. If the medical report says you cannot use your left leg and the customer insists he can, I put my foot down and state, that in traffic you could have a problem. It is yours and the lives of others at stake,' he pointed out. As a result of this painstaking work, Ferro Equip has laid the processes and systems in an organized manner. Further, to strengthen the cause, he willingly shares it with others, who work in modifying cars in other cities.

Earlier, most disabled used tri-cycles. Today, however, many buy cars since modification is a reality. Statistics from the road transport offices reveal, that the number of vehicles registered across various States as 'invalid carriages' have risen four times, over a three year period. The major reason attributed to the same is modified cars. Not only are cars affordable, but there is a wide market of pre-owned cars as well. Further, loans are easily available now. As a result, Ferdinand delivers at least ten to fifteen cars a year. The cost to the customer varies between INR 20,000–40,000. But he states that with the drivers salary averaging around INR 10,000 per month, the modification cost can be recovered in four months. Most importantly, mobility is priceless. Ferdinand has designed car seats for children with cerebral palsy, considering that they cannot sit upright. In fact, these seats can be used anywhere – in the car, on the sofa and even carried outdoors.

Today Ferro Equip has gone beyond car modifications. Ferdinand has designed patient hoists, which are slings to lower the patient from the bed, onto his wheel chair or toilet. The hoist is designed to reduce dependence on expensive care givers. Other innovations include swimming pool hoists, to get into the pool. Designed for children and elders, this is used in institutes like the Paraplegic Centre in Pune, which believes in the healing power of hydrotherapy. In many cases, since the products are import substitutes, the price of Ferro Equip is considerably lower while delivering the same quality.

On weekends, Ferdinand takes children with disability for picnics, to his farm in Niral. He has designed it in an eco-friendly, disabled-friendly manner. The children enjoy outdoor games and the very thrill of having an outing. These days, however, Ferdinand has a new passion. On the drawing board is a recreation cum rehabilitation centre, which shall provide joy to the disabled. A centre where therapy will become fun! He envisions a space with training tracks, water sports, a driving simulator and outdoor games. As he tinkers with the levers and brakes, he dreams about this ambitious venture, which will help the disabled to experience the joy of 'I Can' in their everyday lives.

ADVICE TO OTHERS

1. An entrepreneur should have focus and passion.
2. Viability is critical.
3. You must get joy and thrill from challenges – Enjoy that!

V.R. Ferose

His Indian model of hiring autistic youth went global!

Nilanjan is autistic. Simply put, this means that his communication skills are weak, as compared to others. After high school in the United States, he came to India and did a diploma in special education in Kolkata. His parents heard about the company SAP, which works with autistic youth. He came to Bangalore and made a presentation on 'Open Source Data Systems'. At SAP, he was trained for a year in HAN (High-speed Analytics platform) and secured a seventy-six percentile. Further, he honed his skills in the areas of communication and eMail. Today, he is a confident young man, who goes to SAP meetings and makes independent presentations.

The work with autistic youth at SAP is driven by Ferose; Senior Vice President and Head of Globalisation; SAP AG. Young Ferose is an achiever in the true sense and yet, unlike many successful people, is incredibly modest. At thirty-three years, he was the youngest CEO of a global multi-national company in India. He helped transformed SAP into 'a great place to work for', with a sharp focus on innovation. He was honoured as a 'young global leader' in 2014, by the World Economic Forum. He and his wife, Deepali, were a much sought after couple in India's Silicon Valley. When their only son was one and half years of age, the doctors declared him autistic. Said Ferose, 'My wife decided to drop out of her career and support Vivaan. Being a technology company, my first thought was how can I use technology at all levels – as an enabler, for parents and children. This began my journey in inclusion which has panned out into a global initiative in SAP,' he elucidated.

As he researched on the subject, he came across the inspiring work of Thorkil Sonne; CEO of Specialisterne; a Danish company. The company has eighty per cent of its knowledge workers who are autistic. Thorkil came to the Bangalore SAP and narrated his remarkable journey of setting up this unique company. Like all parents with autistic children, who know organizations do not hire such children, because of their poor social and communication skills, Thorkil began pondering about his son's future. His eureka moment came, when he decided to focus on what his son could do, rather than could not. Some autistic kids are good at music, while others have a remarkable memory and can do repetitive tasks. Leveraging his technology background, he began hiring autistic youth to be a part of a gaming software and testing; a task of repetitive behaviour. Thorkil told Ferose that he had a vision of creating one million jobs for the autistic youth, and this vision could only be fulfilled in a country like India.

Project 'Prayas' was launched at SAP Labs; India. Its focus was on the use of technology for education, employability and engagement of autistic individuals. It began with volunteers, who first held workshops with parents, children and educators to understand autism. A computer assisted lab was started with the Autism Society of India in 2011, to which SAP donated i-Pads and computers. A course of six months on reinforced learning was introduced for children between eight to fifteen years. With this experience, the software was slowly developed, based on these special requirements. The next step was hiring! Five youth were hired for software testing and one for globalisation service. As autistic children find it difficult to communicate, an app for communication, titled 'Bol' was developed. It later found its way to the i-tunes family as a free-ware. Finally in 2013, SAP India launched the first online open source learning platform – www. Learn4autism, with a large repository of free learning material, for autistic children.

In SAP, Ferose was recognised as a turnaround leader. In the crucial R&D labs, which was losing money, he had had in a record time of eighteen months, halved attrition rates and stepped up engagement rates. The company secured the 1st rank in the category of 'Employee Satisfaction'. But personally, the work in disability was far more impactful than anything he had done in the corporate world. As Ferose put it aptly, 'I realised each of us is good in something. We have to tap into that and let it bloom!'

Ferose spoke about the SAP journey at the World Economic forum. Inspired by the work in India, SAP announced a global plan to seek out the autistic and hire them across continents. A decision was also taken that 1 per cent of the SAP global workforce would be persons with autism. This meant 650 to 700 across the world. Ferose exclaimed, 'This means, inclusive hiring is not CSR ... but a part of the core business for SAP'. This also, would result in a new thinking – in the way SAP hires, job mapping and so on. Globally, at this juncture, all eyes were on the Indian experience. Added Ferose reflectively, 'It is strange! The West is aware of autism. But we did it in the most difficult of circumstances in India, where there is no awareness of autism! And now, all eyes are on our Indian experience'. Ferose, however, is not content with this. He outlines a grand vision of 'cradle to grave' with seven pillars. The seven pillars are – awareness, advocacy, early assessment & education, employment, holistic learning which includes music, art & life skills, technology & research and assistive learning. 'The real power of this comes, when all seven elements get integrated,' he outlined, before he concluded, 'Well! It is not easy!'

Ferose is a doer, who quotes Walt Disney, 'The way to get started is to quit talking and begin doing!' Surely and steadily, he is moving forward in each of these steps. For example, the World Inclusion Summit started four years back. It invites leaders from different fields – musicians, sports men, educators – with and without disability to congregate in December, in Bangalore. Ferose hopes to make it one of the largest inclusion summits, globally. Advocacy of the cause he does personally, either by meeting world leaders or in the form of writing. His co-authored book 'Gifted', profiles fifteen inspiring people with disabilities. In research, India lags behind the West. So Ferose is actively involved in the World Autism Research Trust; keeping abreast of the latest. His dream is to create the largest platform that fosters diversity and inclusion in the society. He aims at inspiring ten million lives in the journey of inclusion, by 2020.

Amidst his hectic schedule in the United States, he is busy planning his next book on leadership – 'Defining Moments'. Said Ferose reflectively, 'I realise a lifetime is not enough to do all this. Life takes its own shape and mission. I hope to create a dent in the universe!' I place my convictions in his!

ADVICE TO OTHERS

1. We have to keep long-term benefits in mind. We cannot measure success in the short term.
2. More often, the intangible benefits far exceed the tangible ones.
3. Inclusion should be a way of life, and not a 'project'. The spirit of how the disabled people (or any different people) are included in the workspace, is more important than just some numbers.

Guru Salaudin Pasha

He makes Dancing-on-Wheels possible!

The audience is spell-bound by the magical performance. On a gigantic, specially constructed stage, the artistes twirl in perfect rhythm to the Sufi music. They are dervishes; their white gowns masking the wheel-chairs, which propel their movement. The spectacle is unbelievable!

Meet Guru Salaudin Pasha, the man behind the 'Ability Unlimited' movement. He believes that dance heals and extends wings to the disabled. Art and culture for him, is a part of a larger vision to help create a 'disabled-free India'. His sixty member troupe comprises of people from all age brackets – five to forty years. The difference is, the entire troupe is made up of the differently-abled wheel-chair users, hearing and speech impaired, visually-impaired and those with cerebral palsy. Sounds surreal, doesn't it?

Upon being asked on how he taught expressions and hand movements to the blind or rhythm to the hearing impaired; he explained, 'You beat on their hands to get them to feel the rhythm of the body. It is the touch, the feel and the tap technique. I hold the hands of the visually impaired, so that they can touch my face … and see the expressions there. It needs a mountain of patience to teach them to experience the range of feelings – anger, karuna, bibasa, haasya and so on. Those with physical disabilities can see, but they need to understand the dynamics of wheel balance. I have fallen several times and hurt my head, since I have to first sit on the wheel-chair and step into their shoes, to figure out the adaptations and movements'.

'The line between dance and therapy is thin,' he voiced. With autistic and cerebral palsy students, one cannot give up. Like a therapist one has to keep inspiring them relentlessly. 'They sometimes bite my hand and slap my face. But I have non-stop energy of body and mind!' He smiled as he spoke; his eyes exuding kindness. And miracles do happen.

Five-year Zubair came to Guruji, to master the nuances of dancing. He was born with deformities – devoid of hands and legs with barely any torso. Upon seeing the limbless child, his heart sank! However, seeing the spark in the eyes of the child's father, he decided to mentor him.

He began working industriously, to devise a special choreographic technique for Zubair. A unique technique where only his face, eyes and expressions would be in focus. As in all miracles, the efforts paid off manifold. After months of painstaking toil and tears, Zubair played the part of the golden deer in 'Ramayana on Wheels' and a calf in the folklore production – 'A Kind Tiger and a Sincere Cow'. As Zubair's visage came alive on the stage, the audience was mesmerized. The sincerity in his performance was visible; making the audience quiver in delight! That moment onwards, Zubair had found meaning in his existence. And there was no looking back.

Guruji's ancestors were Hakims (Unani physicians) in the court of the Maharaja of Mysore. As a child, when instructed by his grandfather to keep the younger patients busy, while they waited in the queue, Pasha collected the kids and used to teach them Vedic mantras alongside simple yogic postures. The word went around like wildfire – Many of them reported to his grandfather, that his little grandson's exercises were speeding up their recovery process. Thus, the seeds were sown of his journey – of healing the disabled.

In the villages, disability was perceived as a curse. It was common to hear 'Woh andhey ko lao' (Bring that blind), without referring to a name. Likewise, all mentally challenged people looked different and were called 'Pagal' (Mad). The fact that India has a sixty million disabled population, strengthened Guruji's resolve, that he must commit himself to spreading a positive message about the disabled. His conviction has always been that the disabled have abilities, to tens of thousands of people. 'I chose the stage as a medium to address the nation. When they perform, the audience loses sight of their disabilities and is struck by their manifested abilities'. Guruji has equipped himself with a wide range of skills, from classical Bharatnayam to Manipuri Martial Arts, Classical music and Yoga. He has a Masters in Choreography and a Doctorate in 'Dance and Disability'.

All of these are reflected in the productions that are brought to life by the troupe. 'Yoga on Wheels' shows the disabled artists doing various yogic postures, such as 'Shirsasana' and 'Mayurasana' on wheel-chairs. The wheel-chairs whirl to the strains of 'Khwajare Khwaja' – a production for which Guruji went to Istanbul, in a bid to understand Sufism. To get even the most rigid classicists to see and accept his work, he taught his students to do 'Jatis', 'Thermanams' and 'Adavus' on the wheel-chair. 'Even the conservative Tamil audience was moved to tears!'

His troupe of sixty artists with different disabilities has to practice every day. They earn a salary and even get a bonus for the performances. 'This is a job which will take you round the world ... for free!' The troupe has performed in the United Kingdom, the United States, Italy and France. Their most memorable performances have been at the House of Commons in London, for the Royal family of Muscat and in Verona; the romantic city that plays backdrop to Romeo and Juliet.

In India they participate in reality shows, Television serials and product launches. Several companies request Guruji to customize the show for their special events. Since it is important to sensitize younger children, he performs in schools without a fee. He ensures that the school performances are interactive in nature. He is found encouraging children there, to sit on the wheel-chairs. 'I have reached out to about ten lakh children till date. I have always given them the message, that the disabled do not need pity but an opportunity'. His tone is proud as he speaks about the scale of his work.

The troupe is made up of artists who are mostly from poor, rural families. They have been reared in a 'Do not do' culture. This protective culture of the parents, he feels, makes the child even more disabled. Today the artists work in different areas, for other productions to supplement their incomes. These range from handling sound and light to that of rehearsal directors, artistic directors and make-up artists. All these creative fields have helped in boosting their morale. Watching a deaf-mute daughter perform in a production of 'Women in India from 6000 BC to 2000 AD', a mother broke down and cried. She was proud of the fact, that her daughter could single-handedly fight back two hundred British soldiers, for in the house she did not even lift a spoon.

Guruji laments that currently arts and culture are the last page in any special educator's manual. He hopes to document their knowledge and move it to the heart of the manual, thus putting in place what he terms as – 'The therapeutic educational system through Arts-ability!'

The journey is not easy. 'Travelling with the troupe is almost like a nightmare!' for airports, railway stations, trains and buses are not equipped for wheel-chairs. Even the attending staff, whether it is an air-hostesses or a railway conductor are not educated in diversity. They shirk away from making the disabled comfortable. Sad as it is, most auditoriums are also not disabled friendly. Guruji has often had to carry the artists onto the stage to perform. Now, he also designs special props for his productions. Earlier, his family too, was not supportive. Only after he won a string of awards, including the President's Award, did they sit up and realize that he was the only person in the entire world, who was working on such brave productions! 'My artists are my family. We walk together, "Kadam Pe Kadam" through thick and thin!' His eyes sparkled as he philosophized.

ADVICE TO OTHERS

1. Encourage teachers to inspire.
2. Your actions must incorporate creativity, to rejuvenate the latent abilities in the disabled.

Jacqueline Bonnet

A Touch of Creativity!

In the Uday Park shopping complex, amidst a temple and hardware stores, a shop stands tall. It is frequented for its display; the sheer elegance of the products, as they are visible in the show-window. Embroidered cushion covers, colourful elephants and birds; material with appliqué.

Jacqueline Bonnet greeted me with a traditional 'Namaste'. British by birth, she is more Indian than any Indian I have known. She speaks in Telugu and Hindi with ease. Her wares, the intricately designed beauties have been crafted by the disabled. MESH; as the venture is aptly called, stands for Maximising Employment for Security of the Handicapped. Jacqueline, is the force behind the unshakable spirit of the endeavour. Her friends and clients affectionally call her Jackie now. 'While many know that leprosy is curable, there is a stigma attached to leprosy, which makes people avoid contact and avoid employing those affected with it!' she said.

MESH began its work in 1970, in a leprosy colony in the North of Delhi. The focus was on finding work for those affected by leprosy, those who remained unaccepted at large. It also had within its folds, the quest for making educational opportunities available for children; whose parents had leprosy. It began by encouraging them to rear chicken and simultaneously began marketing the broilers. Later, weaving activities were added, as the initiative spread to the neighbouring colonies. Now, MESH buys handicraft products from not just leprosy affected artisans, but other disabled, pan India. Young interns and volunteer designers from abroad offer design support, alongside guidance in all aspects of fair trade. The products are sold in the MESH shops in Delhi and Hyderabad apart from being exported to countries ranging from Korea to Australia, Sweden, Switzerland, UK, Canada and others..

Jackie has had a fascinating personal background. As a young British teenager, in the late 1970's, she wanted to experience the complex Indian society. One that she had read and heard about from her uncles and aunts, posted in India. The youngest among her three siblings, she is a proud daughter of an Army family. As a trained nurse, she came to the Bethany Catholic Colony Leprosy Association in Bapatla; Guntur district; Andhra Pradesh. The colony was set up by an Australian monk in 1964, with the aim to rehabilitate leprosy patients. Jackie took over the administration of the colony and stayed on for over fifteen years. In the beginning, she lived in a simple hut like the others. Slowly and steadily her work stretched beyond care giving. She worked hard to develop the colony and had got about 350 houses built with government aid. These turned out to be a haven for the colony inmates. They developed a school and crèche for the next generation of children, those of the rehabilitated leprosy patients. A United Kingdom charity supported their higher education. Jackie lived with an Indian family, which soon became her adopted family. Her parents had thought this was a passing whim; of her decision to remain in India and make the lepers' colony her home. But Jackie was resolute and had no intentions of returning to her rich parents. Over the years, she had got used to living for others and improving lives around her. This also fulfilled her spiritual yearnings. However, despite an enriching work life, what she missed was her privacy – simple activities like listening to the radio and reading books. The Bethany colony dwellers in Chirala, made textile products and in this, was her initial contact with MESH. When the opportunity arose to lead MESH, she moved to Delhi with her adopted Indian family.

MESH works with 700 artisans with disability or those affected by leprosy. Its operations are extensive, in thirty-seven producer groups, in twelve States – From Chennai; Tamil Nadu, to Jammu and Kashmir. The Blue Mango Trust is organised with systems and infrastructure in place; on the other hand, some societies are small, with just eight to ten weavers, who work from home. News about this innovative work is slowly spreading, as NGO's and artisans find it difficult to keep up with the design requirements of the market and fetch attractive rates for their wares. MESH is a fair price organisation. It is valued, for it pays the artisans in advance; before lifting the merchandize. Recently, MESH was approached by Tariq from Jammu. His family of shawl weavers had had a degenerative muscular disease. As MESH took control of Tariq's troubles, in turn, it got access to exquisite shawls made in classical designs.

For artisans to have sustainable livelihoods, which help them save and invest in their children's education, perennial orders are required. For this, MESH must be in sync with the market requirements, while preserving old designs. A project with IM Soir (Sweden) helped MESH set up an in-house design studio. This helps it source new materials and interpret shade designs sent by overseas buyers. It also helps the team to understand the supply chain. For instance, with the demand for organic cotton growing, they went on a study tour to look at the organic cotton supply chain in Tamil Nadu. 'The design studio sometimes, dabbles with hundred new samples in a year!' said Jackie. Not surprising, International buyers like Daniela Carraba; Oxfam shop; Australia writes, 'It is a pleasure working with producer partners like yourself … who are proactive in submitting new product ranges and showing initiative with innovative product ideas'.

'It is challenging for us,' admitted Jackie, 'as buyers take consignments and wait to sell … before they can release payments!' Volatility in the export market, for example, even the Fair Trade Movement suffered due to the recession in the market last year, affecting the profitability. MESH has hence, developed a wider basket of smaller foreign buyers, whose orders are stable, through the seasons. Smaller village fairs and church *bazaars* are places where MESH merchandise is sold abroad. It sells its products in India through special events, comprising of carnivals and fashion shows. The expat community also has tea sessions in the MESH outlet in Delhi, which leads to fostering deeper relationships with the customers. 'We are looking ahead at e-Commerce options, to sell online!' She expands – her tone positive and promising.

There are lesser known aspects of MESH's work. Most government programs to rehabilitate the beggars have not worked, so policies are framed, where begging has been branded as a criminal activity. The story of Bharat Mata Kusht Ashram is inspiring. Eighteen year old Gurappa from Karnataka, had the first signs of leprosy; which is numbness, pain in the thumb. As the signs became visible, he was shunned by his family. He then took to begging, on the streets of Mahim; Mumbai. When the Shiv Sena decided to expel outsiders during the Emergency, Gurappa travelled without a ticket, walked for miles and settled on a plot of land, near the Faridabad railway station. Soon, others joined him and thus, was born as locals called it, a 'Kodhiyonka basti'. They heard of MESH, which imposed a condition; to quit begging! Since then, Guruappa has never outstretched his palms for alms. MESH has taught him weaving, like it has mentored many others. They all have a bee-line of orders, to make bed-sheets, table-cloths and mattresses. 'We gave them a livelihood,' pointed out Jackie, her eyes moist.

As I sat listening to the stories of twenty-four year old Asha Bharati, from Varanasi, or the recently widowed Esther from the South, I felt my heart surge with emotions. The characters in the stories kept changing and so did their locations. What remained constant in this flux, was the way they were conceived – 'useless and handicapped'! Isn't it then a lovely thought that they are all artisans today, creating products which reach the playroom of a child in Sweden ... or a designer wardrobe in Australia! Some journeys are different and this is the story of one such journey.

ADVICE TO OTHERS

1. Always dream big.
2. Quality and sustainability is the key to success.

Jo Chopra

A Leap into Love!

Jo McGowan Chopra came to India when she was all of twenty-three. Little did she realise, that in the years to come, she would build from scratch, the 'Latika Roy Foundation'. The foundation works with the most vulnerable of disabilities – including children with Down's syndrome and mental retardation.

What is remarkable is the sense of joy and colour, which seeps into your soul when you step into any of the buildings run by the foundation. It is sheer bliss interacting with the staff and the children. Not surprising, a recent donor gave a generous contribution of INR one crore, when she asked for a desperately needed shortfall of eight lakhs. The vivacious energy of Jo's young staff and volunteers, has helped the foundation win the highly competitive 'Vodafone Give Challenge' of 2013.

The beginning of her tryst with disability was little Moy Moy, an infant she and her husband Ravi, adopted in 1989. Two-week-old

Moy Moy was a premature, abandoned baby in a hospital in Dehdradun, with slim survival chances. 'I am an impulsive person by nature,' expressed Jo. Despite having cerebral palsy, Moy Moy slowly learned to walk, talk, dress and feed herself. Then, at the age of five, a degenerative disorder grasped her. As a result, she began to regress rapidly. 'Today, she has profound disabilities. She uses a wheel-chair, eats through a tube and speaks only with her eyes,' sighed Jo. Before her decline, Moy Moy attended a regular school, but by the age of six, she needed to be enrolled in a special institution. None of the existing facilities were to her mother's liking. 'They were not colourful, happy places where you would want to leave a child!' exclaimed Jo.

In 1995, Jo decided to start her own school; 'Karuna Vihar', where mentally challenged children could access academic inputs (related to their extent of disability), learn self management and get behavioural adaptation skills. Jo reminisces that in the beginning, she had put up signage's at various places, around the city. Why! She even had to organise street plays to get parents to send their kids to her school. Who said beginnings were easy? More so, when the chosen path was not a regular one!

Today, the Foundation has grown by leaps and bounds, spreading its horizon to two centres and touching the lives of over hundred children. Karuna Vihar CDC is an intensive therapy and development management program, for children between the ages five and fourteen, having complex special needs. It also provides after-school support, for children with specific learning difficulties. Karuna Vihar Special School is a day school, aimed at children with disability, between the ages of six and fourteen. It helps to mainstream children wherever possible, while offering activity-based education and therapy programs, for those with academic potential.

'All stages of work have evolved out of a felt need,' she expands. Narrating her experiences of getting a disability certificate for Moy Moy, when she turned eight, Jo reminiscences, 'The experience was so humiliating. Not only for Moy Moy … but for me too! No one explained anything. It took three long visits with the child. I thought, if I am educated and confident, how must it be for a rural person!' This triggered the idea of a help desk at the Doon Hospital – Uttarakhand's largest Government medical centre. This help desk has now grown into 'Gubbara' – a new public private partnership, state-of-art, early assessment and diagnostic centre for children under six, with multiple disabilities.

Funded by the National Rural Health Mission, a 'Home Management Week' provides child assessment and diagnosis at an early age. It also provides a free home management plan for families from across the State. In a typical home management week, ten children, together with their parents, participate in an intensive five day workshop. Each day, the focus is on a different area of development. It aims to arrive at a holistic understanding of the strengths and weaknesses of the concerned child. Perhaps, the most important part of the project's impact is, its success in bringing early intervention onto the government agenda. 'Gubbara has carved a special place in the hospital and is now, a part of the itinerary of any senior Government officer from Delhi!' Jo smiles, as she speaks. The impact of Gubbara is beyond Uttarakhand now. A national initiative has just been launched, in which early intervention centres will be established in every district of the country. Meanwhile, she has set up 'Chota Gubbara'; a desk near the maternity ward. This helps social workers establish a rapport with the expecting mothers, where assessments are carried out at the very earliest.

'We worked for several years without government funding … with help from the Tata Trust and Sight Savers Trust, besides individual donors,' she recollects, gratefully. Today, however, 35 per cent of their work is funded through government grants. She explains that partnership with the government is an initiative beyond money; it helps reach the unreached. The Doon hospital tie-up has helped them reach the rural community, those who do not come to the centres located in urban Dehradun. The foundation also works with Anganwadi workers, to help them identify babies and children in their local communities with subtle disabilities. In the early days, she organised workshops for doctors, where the best of the International speakers were flown in; yet the attendance and participation was not encouraging enough.

The government partnership means with one stroke of a pen, the Health Commissioner instructs doctors in primary health centres to participate. Many of them come unwillingly; but leave the interactive sessions transformed. 'The key to kick-start the government system is to help make it work. For instance, if the Anganwadi worker is not treated with respect, how can she treat a child like a plant?' quizzes Jo. Keshav Desiraju; former Health Secretary, has been one of Jo's biggest support-systems. He would emphatically say in every forum, 'The government has all the money; what we don't have is competent people. If you have competent people, we are there'.

The way ahead is in strengthening the government partnership, by placing two trained local women at each block, as a resource in the health centres. Jo is also busy focusing her energy on writing for policy change and creating awareness. She is also raising funds for the new building of 'Latika Roy Foundation'; where all activities dispersed in different buildings will come under a single roof. 'When I look back, our journey began by INR two lakhs, given by Latika Roy; a tremendous woman, to do something for the children'. Latika Vihar was set up for kids, to explore their creativity. It had a library with a neat toy room, all donated generously by friends from the United States. The toys were flown in, free of charge, by the generosity of the airlines. The philosophy was no competition and no pressure; then came Moy Moy.

As Jo recounts about Moy Moy, she says, 'She wasn't meant to be conceived, but she was. She wasn't meant to be born, but she was. She wasn't meant to survive, but she did. She wasn't meant to be our daughter, but she most certainly is! And when it turned out, that she needed a special school, and there was none to be found in our city, it never occurred to any of us, that starting one would be a problem! Now, years later, Moy Moy's school serves hundreds of children and several people have jobs ... and even a purpose in life!'

ADVICE TO OTHERS

1. Miracles are real, as long as we participate in them.
2. All things are possible with faith, love and willingness to leap into the unknown: So just leap.

Kalyani Khona

An unusual non-traditional matchmaker!

She is bubbly, vivacious and excited about her new venture; unfazed by its challenges. Meet Kalyani Khona; a twenty-two year old recent graduate from Mumbai, who has set up 'Wanted Umbrella'. It is India's first urban match-making agency, focussed on helping the disabled, find a life-partner. It doesn't use computer algorithms or horoscopes; instead, it focuses on bringing like-minded people together. As it functions by means of group settings, it provides an opportunity to know the other, more personally. The service is open to all disabled, above the age of twenty-five. Since her research indicated that the disabled spend more time over their laptops and mobiles, she went on to develop a mobile based app, aptly coined – 'Loveability'.

'I decided to set it up, as it bridges a gap in the society. I feel everyone deserves a soul mate; a companion, even if someone is obese or has health issues or even cerebral palsy. My job is to help them find a companion'. She was inspired to begin this venture, when she learned about the difficultly that the differently-abled face, in meeting those interested in matrimony. In a nation of forty million disabled people, statistics reveal that less than 5 per cent of them get married. She firmly believed that no one should be condemned to live a life of loneliness, unless it is by choice. When it came to a choice of names, she did not want the clichéd ones, like Bharat Matrimony. So the first word 'wanted' was assigned, because no one is unwanted or turned away in her marriage bureau and 'umbrella', as it is a symbol of protection. Kalyani knew this work was not easy, as the biggest mind-set is the deep rooted attitude of the society. Before she set up 'Wanted Umbrella', she observed and spoke to several people. She found that those with disability, were unwanted, rejected and sometimes, even regarded as a bad omen. Saddened, she was determined to change this eco-sphere. So, 10–15 per cent of her data-base includes people without disability, those who are willing to marry disabled people, for they have experienced it in some manner. Her real encouragement came from two sources, besides her supportive parents. Prabha Panse, now ninety-three and bed ridden after a fall, had in operation, a match-making centre for disabled people. Panse showed her register, where she charged INR ten from the disabled, who were seeking a partner. She encouraged Kalyani, by telling her that age was on her side and she would enjoy the work. Others like the visually impaired Preeti Monga, who came out of a bad marriage and found a second supportive husband, also showed Kalyani that the work was not impossible.

Kalyani explained that her marriage bureau works quite differently from Bharat Matrimony and other such sites.

Photograph, caste and religion are not important. It is the overall package. Also, privacy is paramount. For example, Wanted Umbrella has registered a son with autism, whose father has a fancy airline job and wants to keep the disability under wraps. As the methodology goes, a profile is created after a careful registration process. The process is free and includes a personal meeting, alongside identity verification. One to one meetings are arranged or even a Skype or telephone call; depending on what both the parties agree upon. It is commendable that absolute confidentiality is maintained throughout the process. After five profiles are given, a fee is charged. The feedback obtained from the clients helps Kalyani understand the trends. For instance, those visually impaired prefer visually impaired partners. Location is of key importance in many cases, as they prefer to be in close proximity to their parents. Wanted Umbrella members can also take part in curated events and group dinners, where they can meet like-minded people but also feel safe and comfortable in an atmosphere that is free of prejudice.

The start-up entrepreneur recently moved to Gurgaon, leaving the comforts of her home. This was in-keeping with her instinct, that networking prospects were better outside. 'I was really lucky,' she gushed, at the thought of finding her work partner; Shika Anand. The latter, had previously worked in Ernst & Young. Shika has a brother with cerebral palsy; so she acts as the 'emotional' part of the venture; while Kalyani is the business part of it. Currently, Wanted Umbrella has 400 profiles, and is steadily growing. 'My other challenge is my age. People say, you are twenty ... how can you find a match when I am forty?' The key to her business is trust. She also realises that her audience is not limited to the sixty million disabled population, but with inclusion in mind, is the 1.8 billion population of India. To access this wider market, she is building a technology platform. This platform shall make the entire process seamless. Loveability – the new mobile app that helps the disabled meet prospective partners. The disabled, looking for a partner can log in with their social media profile. A detailed profile can be created, which mentions the nature of disability, the medication used and so on. To add, even the option to chat is available.

'Nothing daunts me,' says the gutsy Kalyani, even though she admits her savings are now over and she has been raising some funds through the platform of crowd sourcing. 'I feel joyful every morning. It is a bit like wanting to be the first to walk on the moon … You take the risk, but then, there is an excitement in every step closer'.

ADVICE TO OTHERS

1. *Higher Rewards & Profits:* If you are in this niche sector for a long haul – the profits and rewards shall be higher, due to limited supply or competition. Give 1000 days to this unique sector and on the 1001th day, this business will start generating returns.
2. *Product Customization:* The key to scaling up in this market, is to decide, how you want to customise your product and to what extent. Product customisation is directly proportional to increased sales revenue, because different people are dealing with different kinds of disabilities and disorders. Hence, one solution cannot fit all.

3. *Marketing:* If your product is a purple cow, which it would be, if you are in this sector – marketing and advertising your business, is going to be a totally new ball-game. If you are generating value for your customers and striking the right partnerships with various stakeholders; the Government & the corporate houses, be assured that eventually, business will happen.

Niren Chaudhary

Driven by a larger purpose, he created a special brand.

Srikant works at KFC; RK Cinema. This outlet is the first of the 'specially' abled equity store in India. He joined KFC as a junior team manager in 2008. Being a diligent worker, he was consistently chosen as the 'Employee of the month' and 'Employee of the Quarter'. He then played a leadership role, by supporting the stores in implementing sign language. Further, it was under his able leadership, that orientation was prepared for all speech and hearing impaired employees. Today, he has risen in the ranks to be an Assistant Manager of KFC. Needless to say, he is a role model for others with disability; who find it difficult to progress in their career.

Any first time visitor to the KFC; Banjara Hills; Hyderabad, will be surprised to see the speech and hearing impaired youth deftly taking orders. Why! They even excel at servicing, that too with a smile. Customers seemed to be delighted to be spending money and contributing to an organization, which is committed to hiring youth with disability. This trait, which is generally ignored by most organisations, is what sets KFC apart from the milieu. The person behind this spectacular thought process, who looked at the larger holistic picture, is Niren Chaudhary. Niren was recently promoted from being the India Head to the President; heading global operations of KFC; a brand owned by Yum Brands Inc.

Niren returned to India in 2007, after working with Yum Brands Inc for two decades. This stint took him all over the world, including the United States and Europe. Excited to be back, he realized the potential to paint upon a wider canvas and build a big business. However, he knew that India was a country, steeped in varying shades of social challenges. He knew that whatever he would build would need a sense of purpose. Though he was in a haze about the cause he would take up, he was clear about combining ambition and compassion! More so, he wanted to incorporate this at the inception. His perception stemmed from the belief that it would need to become a part of the DNA and the culture of the business. The fact that Yum globally, had a spirit of making a difference strengthened this conviction. 'So I did not know what it would be, but I knew I did not want it to be a mere tick in the box … but something from the heart,' he remarked.

An incident which took place at a franchisee store in Kolkata touched him deeply. On a routine visit, he shook hands with a receptionist, only to realize that she wasn't willing to let go. With gestures, she communicated that being speech and hearing impaired, she was eternally grateful for the job.

Of course, like everyone else, the job had instilled in her, a sense of pride and joy. This image persisted in his mind, even after he returned to Delhi. 'I realised that this is a calling from my heart. This is what we will embrace, in order to make a difference,' said Niren

In the next leadership meeting, he told his team, that as they built the business, they could make a difference in the livelihoods of the hearing impaired. As he narrated his recent experience, the team brainstormed. Finally, they came up with an idea! They proposed that if Yum was an equal opportunity employer, they could plan opening 'special' stores. The idea was radical – invert the world where the hearing employers would be a minority. This meant, that the hearing workers would have to learn, to get along with the disabled, and take up to learning sign-language. To make the speech and hearing impaired comfortable, Yum decided to focus only on this particular disability. However, the platform of equal opportunity also meant that the kitchen had to be redesigned. Hence, they came up with visual alarms instead of audio and visual-cues instead of verbal; in a bid to design communication better. A special training program empowered these youth, by training them on serving customers, order taking and kitchen management. A score of such KFC's were opened initially. They all had a neat signage, which read – 'Special' with 60–70 per cent hearing impaired staff.

'These restaurants are the best run, have smooth operations and the highest consumer matrix. The managers love it, the customers love it – we have innumerable stories of our consumers crying and hugging these boys and girls. So these Special restaurants fit well into our business model,' he elucidated.

The second level of work was the opening of Yum Academies. Yum had 800 outlets. The thought process was simple, that if 10 per cent of the country's population is disabled; that meant 10 per cent of their stores should be special stores. Accordingly, the 20 special outlets had to become 80. The stumbling block however, was the low level of education that the disabled had. For instance, since there are no special schools, the youth enrol in schools without special educators. This results in having a weak educational background. Fuelled by the solution, they opened six Yum academies, aimed at providing these youth with requisite skills, thereby making them employable. The training duration is that of six weeks; free of charge and the youth have no obligation to join the restaurant.

Niren highlighted that the organisation has a spirit of dissatisfaction, which makes them ask the question – 'What next?' They had round table meetings, where he interacted with employees; mentoring them and enquiring, as to what could they do better. The constant theme which came up was that of career progression, of the speech and hearing impaired employees. 'I realised that their disability was not of intellect, nor of ambition. The human spirit aspires to excel. So, if we truly wanted to be an equal opportunity organisation, we had to give them a chance to move up the career ladder and be a restaurant manager'. This set Yum on the path of career progression – on how to train them in supervisory skills. 'The journey of growth from within shall happen this year, with one youth becoming a restaurant manager and four others shift managers,' Niren elucidated.

This three level approach which has evolved, is a comprehensive one – Yum catches them young, renders them employable skills coupled with jobs and has special stores to make them feel comfortable, alongside giving them an opportunity to scale up the career ladder.

Needless to say, the task is rather challenging. Training the speech and hearing impaired youth and making them supervisors, is easier said than done. Other staff needs to be trained in sign language simultaneously. Also, there was a requirement of funding for initiatives like the Yum Academies. 'So challenges are there. But for me, I have had the deepest sense of satisfaction – that, this sense of compassion has spread to remote areas; as we scale over hundred cities without me being there!'

He recounted an incident about his visit to a restaurant in Visakhapatnam. 'The team members of KFC had adopted a special school, which was in a marshy land. They cleaned the marshes, taught the school children to grow a kitchen garden, harvest it and become self-sufficient. What is more remarkable is that they did it outside their work hours, and never spoke about it. I was blown away. Humbled by what they did. They replied, "We did it because we work for a company with a big heart!"' It is then that he realised, that if all the 900 stores can be a force for good in the community and they share the spirit of doing good, this would be an incredible multiplier effect in the corporate India.

His biggest inspiration is his daughter; Aisha and wife; Aditi. For the last eighteen years, Aisha battled with pulmonary fibrosis – a respiratory disease, which makes breathing difficult. Looking at her spirit, potential and talent, despite the pain of losing her, triggered a sense of compassion in the family. Aisha wrote in her book, 'I cannot change my life, but I can change someone else's!' Niren stated that he felt helpless several times and some of this pain is being eased by helping others. Yum Brand Inc won the President's award this year, for its work with the disabled youth.

Handing me a copy of Aisha's book, Niren reflected, 'My dream is … if I cannot control what India is, we can control what Yum India is. So why don't we make our company; the country we wish to see? One which is inclusive of gender, religion and disability is one more dimension.'

ADVICE TO OTHERS

1. Look for a way to integrate disability in your consumer value proposition.
2. Make it work for not only for the consumers, but also employees and share-holders.
3. Create a culture that creates commitment and support for the initiative across the organization.

He plans the world's most silent hotel run by the deaf.

Arnav has cerebral palsy. A job was unimaginable for him, leave alone becoming an employee of a service industry. Today, after three years of on-the-job training, he works for Clever Fox Cafe at Red Fox hotel – a part of the Lemon Tree hotel chain. He does almost all the twenty-six tasks that his peers do, in the food and beverage department. He takes initiatives in certain tasks and is also seen training his colleagues. He now sets the standard for others, by his perfectly aligned table and In-Room dining tray set up. With this newly acquired confidence, he goes to the gym daily and watches all of Shahrukh Khan's movies.

Patu Keswani is a maverick. Most companies which state that they hire people with disability, quite often, do not divulge the numbers they have hired. In sharp contrast to the others, Patu Keswani;

Chairman and Managing Director of the Lemon Tree hotel company stated, 'Of our 3,500 employees, about 15 per cent are those with disability (includes speech and hearing impaired, locomotor disability, Down Syndrome and going forward visually impaired/low vision and autistic). Our goal for 2025, is to take this to 40 per cent'. In fact, he intends to open a hotel in Sector 60; Gurgaon in 2016, where 100 per cent of the workers, including the managers shall either have a disability or be from a poor family. Having an inclusive human resource strategy has not affected his growth or business adversely. Today, Lemon Tree is the third largest player in the hospitality industry, by virtue of owned rooms. The group owns and operates twenty-seven hotels with over 3,000 rooms across sixteen cities in India. By 2018, Lemon Tree will own and operate over 8,000 rooms in sixty hotels across thirty major cities. Presently, Taj is the largest hotelier in the country followed by Oberoi and ITC. Patu plans to make Lemon Tree, the second largest in the country. These statistics make Lemon Tree the undisputed icon in the hospitality industry, for being socially inclusive.

As I sat in his office waiting for him to finish a meeting, I was welcomed by the bark of the adopted Labrador in the Chairman's office. I wondered whether hiring the disabled was related to Patu's experiencing disability in any manner. 'Absolutely not! And I am not doing anyone a favour either,' he added. 'Any CEO,' he points out, 'wants a compelling argument to in-build any new element into his strategy. Hiring people with disability is mandated by the Companies Act; it is good for business, as attrition is less and productivity is higher. Further, it is good for the Country, as their numbers are significant.

The intersection of these three makes it a powerful argument for any company to hire PwDs'. In India, everyone chases the trained manpower of seven to eight million, without thinking out-of-the-box. It is then logical, that an alternative labour pool, comprising of the disabled is created. Equipping them with the required skill-sets, these vulnerable people can be employed and put in jobs where their abilities can be used. This human resource strategy has indeed worked well for the Lemon Tree hotels. To cite an instance, every year the hotel chain is voted as the best 'Great Place to Work'. Across the board, the employees stated they liked the fact that their employer believes in being socially inclusive while doing business. In 2011, it won the NCPEDP MphasiS Universal Design Award. This award recognizes and acknowledges those organizations, which are playing a pivotal role in making life accessible for people with disabilities. This year, Lemon Tree has partnered with NCPEDP (National Council for Promotion of Employment for Disabled People) to constitute an award for organisations and people, promoting consistently employment and empowerment of the disabled. Not surprising, Patu has been chosen to chair the two recently constituted committees, which will steer the disability policies and corresponding work in India. He is the Chairman of the CII National Committee on Special Abilities and the Chairman of the Skill Council for PwD's (SCPwD).

Their first Lemon Tree employee with disability was in kitchen stewarding, as this area did not have customer interaction. 'Recently, a woman stepped out of a limousine and gave me a wedding card. I did not realise that our employee was from an affluent family and yet, could not get a job because of disability. Once he was employed, the respectability gave him status in the society to marry and live an independent life,' said Patu, highlighting some of the unexpected benefits that the disabled youth get, when they are in a good job. This social mobility is possible because of a job – one which empowers a disabled. This sense of empowerment is what drives them to ensure that Lemon Tree is an equal opportunity employer. For Patu, clearly it's not about charity. 'There is no sense of charity, because I think that's what kills somebody's self-dignity.' Lemon Tree recruits boys and girls from NGO's across States and institutes like the Institute of Hospitality Management. The training and induction module for all new recruits, whatever be the level, includes sensitization and awareness towards PwDs. Those hired are taught the skills and technical qualifications so required for their roles. The managers patiently ensure that the disabled youth meet the exacting service standards. This involves some degree of extra effort and expertise, like partnerships, to convert training modules into sign language courses, for the hearing impaired. Further, all the staff go through a crash course in sign language.

Patu points out, that in India there are no social networks of the disabled, which can help them get employed like other caste or alumni networks. Unemployment automatically converts to higher poverty levels. Yet, given the correct ecosphere and trainings, their abilities come to the fore. Aradhana Lal, Vice President, Sustainability, remarks, 'We treat them with respect and dignity and give them decent wages'. This inclusive employment mantra implemented across the hotel chain gives him the greatest satisfaction. Gradually, from kitchen stewarding, the hotel tried placing the disabled in the food and beverage operations, alongside housekeeping. 'When food and beverage section says they have too many youth with disability, then I just move on to another operational manager. There is no question of "I can't", as when the managers are hired they are told right in the beginning, that we are an equal opportunity employer,' states Patu, who ensures this clear message of inclusion trickles down to all levels. While Lemon Tree began with locomotor disability, today those with hearing impairment, dominate the workforce. Aradhana explained that now, they have stretched their hiring to take youth with cerebral palsy. 'We are working with an NGO to understand this disability and the learning process involved,' said she. Even as in their pilot, youth with cerebral palsy serve water and change tables in the coffee shop at Red Fox; Gurgaon.

An IIT Delhi, IIM Kolkata and Tata Administrative Services alumnus, Patu worked with the Taj Group of Hotels for eighteen years, followed by a stint in AT Kearney, as a consultant. His mother was a doctor in the Indian Army and father was a railway engineer. The consulting stint brought in some money, so he decided to set up a mid-scale hotel in 2002–2003, on a plot of land in Gurgaon, with plans of relaxing and retiring early. Four years and four hotels later, a private equity firm valued the chain at INR 800 crores, against his mentally calculated conservative evaluation of INR 300 crores. From there, the vision kept evolving and expanding. The one comfortable hotel in Gurgaon expanded to the Lemon Tree Group – Lemon Tree Premier; an upscale brand. Lemon Tree Premier; A four-star plus hotel providing five star services, Lemon Tree Hotel; a midscale brand and Red Fox Hotels; an economy brand. The chain kept expanding across India, with healthy top-line and bottom-line growth. Further, there was an infusion of consortium capital by the United States based PE firm – Warburg Pincus, the Dutch Pension Fund Manager – APG, the India based Real Estate Fund – Kotak Realty Fund and the Japanese financial institution – Shinsei Bank.

Next on the drawing board is his Magnum Opus; a hotel near the golf course in Gurgaon, which will be completely manned by managers and workers from economically weaker families and with disabilities. 'Sign language is like Chinese and Russian. Both make sounds but we do not understand it, till we learn it. Imagine, this will be the quietest hotel in the world,' he remarked. And it will undoubtedly give its guests, a uniquely unbeatable experience!

While Patu comes across as empathetic and inclusive, it was indeed not easy for him to integrate these principles into a profit-driven business model. The hotel industry thrives on customer satisfaction. Is it difficult to marry diversity and service? 'We never ask – "Is it possible?" We are adventurous. We may fail the first time and succeed in the next!' Remarked Patu, reminding us that failure too, helps step up the ladder of success and this is the true essence of entrepreneurship.

ADVICE TO OTHERS

1. The CEO has to walk the talk.
2. Have persistence of purpose.
3. Break the barriers, beat your head till it works. *'Lage raho, lage raho'* is his mantra.

Shilpi Kapoor

She believes in connecting the worlds of disability and technology.

'Technology is the key to inclusion!' is the mantra of this feisty, forty plus Shilpi Kapoor. She is a self-taught technologist. Her passion for disability, sprung from an unexpected event, which came quite early in her life. She was tracking network security and hackers for a firm in the United States. 'In this field, speed is the essence,' she explained. In her early work life, her boss, based out of Washington DC, was pleasantly surprised when he learnt that Shilpi had found and apprehended a hacker in record time, even before he could do so. Her superior was incredibly fast in his work; always a few steps ahead of her and had taught her the ropes of network security. Shilpi had made him proud as a mentor. When she quizzed him on why he had responded late for this case, his reply came as a shock! He told her that he was wheel-chair bound, paralyzed neck down. That he operated the computer by using a puff-and-blow technique. 'I had worked with him for two years. His having a disability never cropped up!' This was in 1995. She decided this was her path – of making a difference by using technology for the disabled.

While she was still looking for the big idea, she happened to visit the Royal National Institute of Blind in London, which had a screen-reading technology for the blind. This converts the text on a computer screen, to sound, enabling the blind to read. The cost was INR 1.5 lakhs, versus the existing imported Jaws technology which was available in India for $1,000. She borrowed money from her grandfather, who asked her not to repay the loan, if she taught one blind boy free. She found two blind boys in her neighbourhood and coached them on Saturdays. She also wrote a manual on how to impart computer education to the blind. Her friends, who dropped in, encouraged her to scale up the endeavour. So, in 1997, she set up the country's first visual impairment training centre at Churchgate; Mumbai. Mumbai University gave her the space to install five computers. Some funding was given by the National Association of Blind and the Gates foundation. 'I always believe nothing should be given free,' she remarked thoughtfully. A nominal fee of INR 2,000 was charged for a six months training and the fee returned to the top three achievers. The challenge she faced was, that the blind boys could not get jobs, despite the good training. Or those who were telephone operators remained so, bereft of better prospects. This taught her two lessons. One was that organizations had deep mindsets on hiring the blind, which could not be surmounted easily. This was an indication that her training would not result in a placement. The second lesson was that skilling appeared to be a not-for-profit domain, though her interest was in a for-profit area. Hence, she needed to look beyond skilling.

BarrierBreak Technologies was born by creating a win-win situation, of working on outsourced technology solutions by hiring the disabled. 'Of course, I had no seed money. My father said, "Make money first and then risk it",' she smiled as she spoke. She did technical writing of curriculum for skilling companies like Aptech, NIIT and Jetking, leveraging her computer training expertise. She began BarrierBreak in 2008, with a team of twenty-five and all had some form of disability. The idea was rather simple. Many Indian companies were offering software solutions to the US market, which had to conform to the US Discrimination Act, which mandated that all software be disabled-friendly. So, she decided BarrierBreak could test services for accessibility, before they went to the market. The market was rather large, pegged at $12 billion. Venture capitalist; Vineet Rai of Aavishkar was sold on the business plan and promptly invested in BarrierBreak. Unfortunately, the venture did not do well. The challenge was that the Indian companies were not interested in conforming to this discrimination clause stipulated in the Act. They wanted to deal with it, only if the issue was raised by their customer. 'I realised I had to survive! Aavishkar was breathing down our neck. I had people ... but no revenue. Those were interesting times'.

She smartly switched markets, deciding to focus on US companies, in the absence of the Indian market. This gave a fresh lease to the endeavour. Today, BarrierBreak operates in nine countries, offering services ranging from accessibility testing to digital books, digitising content for universities and libraries and making accessible videos. 'In fact, anything in technology which involves fixing and making disabled-friendly things,' she expanded. This can range from bank ATM's to health products, like diabetic testing. Another focus area is an advocacy to sensitise the government to make their websites accessible and more recently; to implement the concept of a universal design. 'Even though the Government has fixed targets, for their websites becoming accessible, after incessant lobbying by disability groups, very little is being done,' she lamented.

Today, BarrierBreak has a staff of eighty, with 75 per cent being disabled. This ranges from autism to visual & hearing impairment and includes locomotor disability. 'It's fun to see how different disabilities support each other!' For instance, the hearing-impaired make e-books for the blind. The disabled come with little qualifications and work experience. Knowledge of English and being logical is a prerequisite to being hired. BarrierBreak invests in their skills by understanding their disability.

Shilpi admitted that not getting a ready pool of trained manpower was a challenge in the early days. They turned it to their advantage by training these youth, since the organisation understood disability. 'Personally for me, it is gratifying that I don't have to look for placements now. I train and hire them. And this makes us a uniquely "by the disabled, for the disabled" company,' she emoted proudly. The company has a supportive eco-sphere, one which mentors differences – whether in appearance or disability. All the employees learn the sign language quickly, without going through formal classes.

Till a universal design is mainstreamed, the disabled in India shall need assistive technology products. To cite an example – a colour coded keyboard is required by a dyslexic child for reading purpose. In India, she finds that most research and development products remain prototypes and do not get marketed. Sensing a gap, BarrierBreak imports assistive technology devices, by negotiating sensible price points for the Indian customers. Techshare exhibitions are held in the metros, which has helped the government and the disability related NGO's to realise the power of technology. This business has grown and now has a helpline within its folds. It also has in place, a dealer network, spanning six cities. Schools and colleges are the main catchment areas at present. Barrierbreak has a turnover of INR 4.5 crores and is into profit making. Another feather in their cap is accredited to their buying back of shares last year, from their investor; Aavishkar.

Soon to be launched is a mobile based application, to help ease mobility and navigation. 'For India, the way forward is community based resources,' she remarked, while narrating her dream to set up three model libraries, aimed at complete accessibility.

ADVICE TO OTHERS

1. Understand disability. Don't make assumptions.
2. Disability can be a business.
3. Technology is the driver for inclusion.

Art with a Heart!

'It's easy to make a buck. It's a lot tougher to make a difference!' – Tom Brokaw

At twenty-three, as a recent graduate, Smriti Nagpal set up Atulyakala; a social enterprise that works with deaf artists. 'Let your hands do the talking' is the tagline. Sign language came naturally to her, having grown up with deaf siblings. Founding Atulyakala, which when translated means 'unparalleled art', had a vision – to provide creative opportunities to the deaf artisans. 'We are linking social consciousness with design and breaking out from classic models of business, to create an enterprise with a difference. At Atulyakala, we are co-creating with differently-abled artists, who we believe are talented and awesome. We are young, fun and persistent,' she smiled, notwithstanding the myriad challenges of a start-up.

Nagpal's older siblings are both hearing-impaired. Her sister lost her hearing ability, as a baby and her brother, when he was all of ten. Sign language, hence, became a mother tongue for Smriti; the youngest in the family. She took up the charge of acting as a bridge between her parents and siblings. When she was sixteen, the Secretary of the National Association of the Deaf asked her if she would interpret for the World Disability Day. 'I was just thrown into it! An audience of 10,000; ministers standing next to me,' she gushed at the memory. But this event opened up new opportunities for her – such as travelling to Seoul for the AbOlympics amidst other things. And then, when she was in her second year of graduation, she began doing the morning news bulletin for the hearing impaired, on the Doordarshan television network. After college, her father suggested she join the family business, dealing in fitness equipment. 'But every day, I felt I should be doing something I love; some activity around sign language which is so integral to me!' Her life goals were clear to her. One day when she was out with her sister, speaking in sign language, she met Amit Vardhan; a talented deaf artist who was languishing in a dead-end job. He told her candidly, 'Can you take me out of this monotonous work that I do for an NGO, which is making folders all day? I love to paint!' Smriti approached Harshit, who like Amit also studied at Delhi's College of Arts and told him, 'I have this idea buzzing in my head. Will you join?'

Today, Atulyakala's core team is made up of Smriti, Harshit and Amit, along with Pinto and Uday. Pinto; a hearing-impaired photographer, also had the creative urge but was lacking the right place to learn and grow. Born into an orphanage in Kolkata, he eventually became a helper at the American Embassy; Delhi. He used all his savings to buy a camera and a laptop and taught himself photography. Most weekends witness him scurrying away to different locales, taking photographs all over the country; from Port Blair to Kanyakumari.

India is home to several million hearing-impaired people, estimated to be between ten to fifteen million. Perhaps, on the global map, one out of every five hearing impaired is in India. Yet, there are numerous problems faced by the deaf community. Lack of education is the biggest hurdle. For them, there are just two ways to communicate – through writing or sign language. Since there are no special educators in most Indian schools, deaf students cannot understand the lessons. Most of them spend time in school creatively; drawing and painting. There is a large pool of talent but because they are not technology or communication savvy, they languish around, doing mundane tasks like making a hundred files, a day.

When compared with their peers, it is note-worthy, that the deaf students, while leaving school, are invariably far behind academically. In fact, they even lack basic literacy at times. This gap is further widened by the fact, that there are few or no higher educational opportunities, for the hearing impaired in India. Most schools are limited till the tenth standard itself. The lack of deaf graduates leads to a lack in the number of qualified deaf teachers, resulting in spiralling down of educational opportunities of the hearing impaired. It hence, becomes a vicious cycle.

Team Atulyakala wants to bridge the gap between the deaf and the hearing communities. They are focussed on creating a space which celebrates, explores and represents deaf art culture in India. They also hope to increase awareness about Indian Sign Language; further exploring its creative side.

Smriti is passionate about bringing together artists, who can hear and those who cannot. Deaf artists are isolated in more ways than one. She firmly believes that learning, interacting and creating designs along with mainstream artists is an enriching experience, nurturing both sides. Like all youngsters, team Atulyakala is tech savvy and uses the new tools of social media, for hearing the impaired artists can build up relationships that are more meaningful.

To cite an example, Amit now draws portraits of fellow passengers on the metro, using a tablet, rather than the hand-drawn sketches that he had done before. Using the tablet, he e-Mails copies of his sketches out to anyone who requests them. He has now become a 'metro hero', having hundreds of friends on Facebook. Amit *bhaiya*, as he is called, also holds caricature lessons. Based on this experience, Atulyakala offers this service of teaching deaf artists on using Instagram and other on-line tech forums, to help them build a portfolio and reach out to a wider audience.

Though young, Atulyakala has commissioned several art projects including working with the National Association of the Deaf's peace walk. The design team at Atulyakala, want their customers to not just have cool products, but to feel a connection with the hearing impaired artists. They also want to ensure that the artists have a chance to express their innate creativity and not be constrained into doing what amounts to manual, mechanical work.

Atulyakala has designed its entire process and brand, around the usage of sign language. They hold interactive workshops in schools, colleges and cafes, where alphabets in sign language are taught. They even hand out small tokens like book-marks in these workshops. Simple sign language is taught –

such as showing the participants, as how to sign their names and how to sign 'love' in sign language. Their current projects include – creating products inspired by the signs in the Indian Sign Language; exploring the creative aspect of it and creating a niche in the market for the products. 'Silent Experiences – Conversations with Deaf Artists' is an ongoing series of interviews, with artistes to tell others about the untold stories and experiences of talented deaf artists in India. For more interaction, a Facebook page has been created; 'Community of Human Sign Language', where the hearing impaired shared their trials. At the same time, they can listen to others like them.

Some break-throughs have happened. The products are on Craftsville and Good will stories. Recently, they have reached Denmark. However, like any young enterprise, Atulyakala faces the challenges of investment and need for working capital. Also, deaf artists want a regular salary which the young company cannot afford presently. Smriti feels that she cannot let down those artists, who call upon her, from different parts of India. She hopes to mainstream Deaf Art like in Europe and United States, where it is recognised as a part of the regular art scene.

ADVICE TO OTHERS

1. Never give up on your dreams. It's important for the youth to dream and follow their heart.
2. You don't have to be a social entrepreneur. Simply do small things for people every day and experience the happiness.

Sugandha Sukrutaraj

Intellectually challenged become computer savvy.

Sandeep was rolling textiles in a retail shop. He was slapped and abused each time he made a mistake. For this, he earned a mere salary of INR 350 monthly. His parents had no other options, since they didn't know anyone who would give their low IQ child, a job. Today, he fills customer application forms and has the respectability of being a white collared, IT worker.

When you encounter AMBA; operating from a large rambling house, nestled amidst trees, you tend to feel nostalgic. It is a slice of the old Bangalore and history, for it also happens to be the Nobel Prize winner; Sir C V Raman's house. Today it is home to AMBA; an initiative to empower and mainstream the intellectually challenged, by giving them low-skill IT jobs.

'Nearly 3 per cent of the population has intellectual deficiencies; that means it affects the lives of thirty-five million Indians. These are the most neglected in the society. Schools don't know how to handle them. So they drop out. Institutions don't know what to do with them, after they turn sixteen. Their number is large and needs a holistic solution,' remarked Sugandha Sukrutaraj; the force behind AMBA. She decided to provide employment opportunities to these youth, in a focussed manner. Setting up this organisation, where the work is presented to others, not as charity but as a business opportunity, has not been easy for Sugandha. Today at sixty, having lost two husbands to cancer and having to bring up two children single-handedly, she admitted it is the transformational impact of the work which keeps her going. AMBA is now a decade old and has evolved into collaborative 'learn and earn' centres called AMBA Centres for Economic Empowerment of Intellectually Challenged (CEEIC's).

The thought that triggered this work was simple. Everyone likes to say they are from the IT world, because it bestows a certain degree of attention and respectability. So why not link the intellectually challenged to the IT domain? Today in AMBA, the intellectually-challenged people with IQ below sixty, are trained to operate computers and are rendering their services doing online data entry. The result is not just sustainable livelihoods but a change in the attitude of the wider society, towards the intellectually challenged. 'Now, we don't have to talk about mental disabilities. Their parents are full of pride, as their children with the lowest IQ are all computer operators,' she stated proudly.

In Jamnagar; Gujarat, Sugandha had helped bring out a quarterly magazine in Braille, which was distributed to schools on a national platform. Her organisational abilities came to the forefront as the Regional Manager; CONVEX, the first International exposition on Aerospace and Aviation in India in 1993. Her other mainstream work was the Chief Executive Corporate Liaison; Deccan Aviation and as a programme director on contract, with the Department of Information Technology; Government of Karnataka.

Her experience of being on the core committee and the board of the Special Olympics, gave her deeper insight into the hidden talent of the disabled. Some of the initiatives they undertook were the training of 640 trainers according to the norms of Sarva Shiksha Abhiyan. These trainers in turn, went as special educators to schools, for children with intellectual disabilities. Then, in 2003, 110 youth participated in the Special Olympics in Ireland and thirty-seven of them came back with gold medals.

Sugandha has no formal higher education but she understood computers. Thus, AMBA Centre for Economic Empowerment of Intellectually-Challenged Adults (AMBA CEEIC) came into being as a Trust, to work with these special children. Initially, the expenses were kept low. The Air Force infrastructure and special educators were used for the program. She found youth with cognitive impairment, unemployed or exploited in their work and brought them to the centre. Over the first three years, about sixty youngsters were brought in and trained in simple processes. But it was a visit to Jeevodaya in Nagpur, which works with 300 kids with intellectual disability that oriented Sugandha to a process of learning, which AMBA adopted in their learning centre.

The key was to develop the intellectual challenged person's

visual functions. The trainees begin with no knowledge of ABC. Even after the training they may not know ABC, but they recognise the shapes. So the process of learning, now templated, is a process of matching and reinforcing the images of alphabets in various ways like games, using cut-outs and so on.

'There are three cycles of repetition,' Dinakar remarked. He had left his monotonous telecom job to join AMBA as its Operational Head. 'In this period, they observe, soak and retain.' The next three months focus on practising the usage of the computer key-board. Peer to peer learning for correcting errors has been found to be the most effective method of learning. The training is free of cost. In the three months on-the job, they earn INR 500 and while working on assignments, the salaries range from INR 1,000–INR 5,000 a month.

'We bypass formal mainstream learning, slowly increasing the degree of difficulty and in about six months, they collectively outflow low skill back – office work to include visual data entry, mail-merging, scanning and dispatch,' Sugandha explained. 'Individual attention is also necessary in the beginning, to assess and give inputs, according to the degree of intellectual disability'.

When Sugandha realised that her team could do repetitive jobs like data entry, their first assignment came from Tata Teleservices, to do their yellow forms. For this work, the entire training had to be designed around typing, editing, folding and then posting. The work was started with ten kids with intellectual disabilities and ten volunteers. There was no sympathy, for work timings had to be adhered to rather strictly. If there were deadlines, everyone had to work on weekends and put in longer hours. Tata Teleservices was followed by work from other telecom providers like Idea cellular and Airtel Cellular, for eight years during the telecom boom period. Today, they serve a wide spectrum of industries like hotels, ice cream, insurance and market research. Said Dinakar, 'Yes, their speed was one-fifth of a normal child. But they work in a focussed manner and the work is amazing … with 100 per cent accuracy'.

The success of working with the telecom sector has spurred AMBA to look for other companies to outsource their back-office work. Intel, Ujjivan, Special Olympics Bharat, Dinshaw's Ice cream, the electronics division of Karnataka and Sarva Shiksha Abhiyan have been partners. In the process, AMBA has evolved a model for scale. The intellectually challenged community does not have the social skills to work in a mainstream environment. Their delayed milestones, limited cognitive skills, inability to go through formal education and speak for themselves, requires special attention. So the scale is achieved by partnering with organisations which work with intellectually disabled children. Three youth from each centre come for training at AMBA. They in turn, train others through the peer-to-peer education method. 'For smaller NGO's, we do have to give computers and help them access some work, till they can tap into the local business,' elucidated Sugandha.

In a hostile atmosphere, where the society keeps these vulnerable children hidden, since they look and act different, AMBA comes as an oasis of joy and security. Remarked a mother who had accompanied her son, 'He was paralysed for a year. Every day he asked, "When can I start going to AMBA?"' Priya, their trainer, with an intellectual disability, recently won the CII Women's Exemplar Award. Priya struggled in a mainstream school till the seventh grade; ridiculed and ignored by the teachers and the students alike. At AMBA, they recognised her desire to constantly reach out and help others. One day, when a special educator did not turn up, Priya pitched in, to resolve the crisis. Today, she trains new recruits and actively helps in calming and modifying the aggressive nature, of some of the kids. Ravi Kiran who had an IQ of eleven has improved to sixty, over a four-year period, astonishing even the doctors at NIMHANS. Roselin, who was once home bound, now commutes by two buses with a spirit of independence. Sugandha's current plans are to establish centres in rural India. Mind Tree has helped set up three in Andhra Pradesh, donating computers. A large order from CMIE and the team is busy looking for volunteer software engineers, to convert the forms. Plans include incorporating a company owned by the AMBA Trust, akin to the Tata model. Sugandha has won accolades for her work, ranging from the Ashoka Fellowship to the Intel prize. On the drawing board is an International event, to raise funds and create a corpus for the company. The vision for the future is to create sparks, which will serve as catalysts for organic growth.

ADVICE TO OTHERS

1. Quoted Bill Drayton; Founder, Ashoka, Innovators for the Public: Social entrepreneurs are not content with just giving a fish or teaching how to fish. They will not rest until they have revolutionised the fishing industry.

Upasana Makati

The founder of the first Braille lifestyle magazine.

At just twenty-five, Upasana Makati; a young public relations professional, found herself wanting more from life. Not completely satisfied with her well-paying job, she realised that what she was looking for, was something different. Something, that would make her happy, which she could run by herself. The result was White Print; India's first ever lifestyle magazine in Braille, for the visually impaired.

A common question posed to Upasana is, did she have empathy for the disabled, because of experiencing the challenges of disability in her own family? 'I wasn't even remotely connected with visually impaired people before "White Print"'. It was born out of a thought, which kept nagging at me, while I was doing my routine work. Somehow, it was difficult for me to digest, that the visually impaired didn't have a monthly magazine of this nature in Braille – that would reach their doorstep each month,' she remarked. 'Every one of us, want to get up and read a newspaper or curl up in bed, with a book. But nothing like this existed for the blind. Their mother or father had to read from a book or they had to listen to audio books or radio,' she added. Her idea was strengthened by the fact, that India has the largest number of visually impaired in the world and many of them are literate. 'It is paradoxical,' she remarked, 'that those of us, who can see and read are spoiled for choice, when it comes to reading material; yet sections of the society like the visually impaired had no choice at all'. She spent three months researching, which included talking to various blind people and institutions which trained them. Armed with enormous personal drive and ambition, she gave up the mundane task of her corporate job. Then she set up White Print; India's first lifestyle magazine in Braille!

Like any life-style magazine, White Print covers a wide range of topics, from food to politics, as well as inspirational stories and profiles of successful people. Inside is music, audio and book reviews, pieces on arts and culture as well as International issues. Barkha Dutt has a political column and now readers can contribute poetry and articles. Upasana does the coordination, curation and compilation of the magazine herself. She uses a Braille-translation software called Duxberry to convert the articles written in MS Word to Braille. 'It is like a one woman army,' she recounts, though friends and family do pitch in. For proof-reading, she employs a person fluent in Braille, to read it before the final copy is sent out to print, at National Association of Blind (NAB). Thereafter, the copies are posted to the subscribers. There are no postal charges, since it is a publication for the visually impaired. Priced at INR thirty for a sixty-four page copy; White Print has subscribers from all over the country. The magazine goes to libraries, NGO's and individual subscribers. Maximum subscription is from South India. Satisfaction comes from the fact that people from even the smaller metros are on their subscription list.

Being in Braille, the magazine is completely made up of text, with no images or pictures. This makes it a challenge to find advertisers, who are willing to break out of their traditional visual-heavy way of doing business. 'Advertisers find it challenging, as they cannot convert their logos into Braille or even convert their strategy to this new medium,' she rues. Raymond was the first advertiser that took a chance with advertising in White Print. They, in fact, did a five page advertorial. Tata and Aircel too pitched in. Coca Cola was the first to use the medium innovatively, by designing a musical advertisement, for which White Print inserted a chip into each magazine.

Upasana was clear when setting up her venture, that she would not go the charity way, but set up a sustainable business with revenues. This meant that she had to step up the advertisement and subscription base. She has approached the government, which initially told her that there were no guidelines about advertising in a magazine for the visually impaired. 'I am working on this and shall make a breakthrough soon,' she said, her voice resonating determination. Unperturbed by the challenges, what makes her hopeful, are the statistics – India has fifty-six lakhs literate individuals today. As I look at her, I wonder – were her parents supportive of their young daughter; fresh with a communication degree from Canada, sinking her one year's earnings into an unusual venture? She smiles at my question and happily replies, 'They see me happy. Also my parents felt, that since I was young, this was a good time for me to experiment and follow my heart!' This rock-solid support has helped her through the early entrepreneurial struggles.

In India, it is not easy to set up an enterprise. These roadblocks have not deterred her from her path. Registration of the name itself, took eight months, with two rejections. Finally 'White Print' was accepted and launched in 2013. While revenues are trickling in slowly, what keeps her enthusiasm going is the response from the readers. She measures her success by the warm feedback and unusual calls she receives every day. One young girl said, that she read the magazine cover to cover from morning to evening. Another reader wrote that she spent the time on the Mumbai train reading White Print, rather than listening to the radio. Poems, seven page long letters of appreciation amidst other notes have poured in. 'I would one day, like to have a visual impaired team working with me … doing the writing and helping with the creatives,' she beamed with pleasure, outlining her future inclusive vision.

Having tasted the joy of reaching out to a neglected but large community, Upasana is looking beyond White Print. A small musical video – 'B for Braille' was made, with Upasana singing the background score and put on YouTube. This is to spread the message that learning Braille is important. White Print celebrated its first year and launched a copy each month, consistently. White Print has started an editorial association with the Caravan Magazine, which allows her to expand her reportage. Laurels have come her way like the L'Oreal Paris Femina Women Awards 2014 for Science & Innovation. Sharing her future life goals, she states, 'Maybe an International edition of White Print!'

ADVICE TO OTHERS

1. Do not hesitate to do anything new.
2. Combine a social cause with an idea.

Vidhya Rammasuban

Providing transport solutions to the disabled.

Deepa Maski, a wheel-chair user, now attends all family functions and social gatherings – a feat made possible by Kickstart cab service. 'The best part is, before I needed to stay close to the office, since my motorised wheel-chair can take me ten kilometres. Now my work in Wipro has shifted, but I did not need to shift our residence. I can wheel my chair and sit in their cab and wheel myself out without assistance,' she said, her eyes lit. This gives Deepa, a great sense of freedom and a fresh lease of life.

I had first heard of Vidhya's earlier entrepreneurial venture; Himalaya-on-wheels which was a bold and ambitious project, with the local disability group – Peoples Action Group for Inclusion & Rights (PAGIR), to attract tourists with disability to Ladakh. She ensured that some tourist spots and hotels are accessible, and then went on to marketing it, as an 'inclusive' destination. It was not surprising then, that her next venture in her home-town Bangalore, also deals with helping the disabled commute with comfort. Have you ever tried to travel in a car with a friend or relative on a wheel-chair? Or to take an old parent to the hospital? Or if you are hearing impaired and only use sign language, tried calling a cab? These are issues which troubled Vidhya. Her solution was – Kickstart Cabs; a service that helps the disabled commute with comfort. The name 'Kick start' was coined, as both; an enterprise and engine are kick started. Vidhya has worked extensively in Uttaranchal and in Nepal, with rural communities, to help them find their own solutions for livelihood. 'A common thread in my work has been disability,' said Vidhya, who returned to Bangalore, to begin her entrepreneurial journey. She had a strong belief that giving transport solutions to the have-nots helps them access employment, recreation, information and thus, helps create an equitable society.

Vidhya reeled facts and figures to indicate the size of the market and the viability of this socially inclusive idea. Census data of 2001, shows that there are approximately six lakh people with disabilities and about seven lakh senior citizens in Bangalore. Assuming about 10 per cent of this population will be city potential cab users, the numbers are 1,30,000. They did a survey, where 96 per cent of people with disabilities responded. Market research indicated that they need accessible transport services. And 62 per cent felt this was so essential, that they were willing to pay a premium on the price. Doctors in hospitals narrated cases with spinal injuries, which had dropped out of their rehabilitation visits, owing to harrowing transportation experiences. These facts strengthened her plan, to provide personalized and accessible transport that would be comfortable to those with mobility restrictions. A service with remodelled cars, that provided comfort in seating and facilitated the entry and exit from vehicles made imminent sense.

Vidhya's partner for this venture was Ankit Jindal; a visually impaired Wipro employee, who complemented her skills with his great business acumen. Ankit had set up a social enterprise; Diversity and Equal Opportunity Centre (DEOC), dedicated to making workplaces more inclusive. As a person with 90 per cent loss of vision, he himself experienced the difficulties in commuting, in the unruly Bangalore traffic. He strongly believed that the Himalaya-on-Wheels concept was needed on the plains. KickStart was a part of Ankit's effort, in giving back to the community of the disabled. The initial investment came from pooling their own savings, coupled with some initial funding from Mphasis; a company known for supporting disability causes. A mid-size Bangalore based software company, owned by Hewlett Packard, Mphasis uses its corporate social responsibility funds to support disability causes. Ganesh Ayyar; Chief Executive Officer; Mphasis said in the flag-off event, that KickStart is a much required service that provides freedom, mobility and dignity to those who may need support. 'MphasiS continues to look for more such avenues that support socially vulnerable groups,' he observed emphatically in the launch event.

The beginnings were small. Three cars modified to different needs. The first car; a Swift Dzire, has a swivel chair that can come half way out of the front door. This enables a person with crutches, a walking stick or one on a wheel-chair to move onto the car seat. The second model; a Wagon R has a ramp facility, so that a wheel-chair can be wheeled in and secured into the car. The third model; a Toyota Liva, has a detachable seat that can be converted into a wheel-chair. The modifications, explains Vidhya are expensive. They vary between INR 20,000 to INR three lakhs. Some need imported parts. So, one concern area to be addressed by them is aimed at lowering these costs.

The response has been overwhelming. The three has expanded to four cars. Currently, the overheads have been kept low, with Vidhya handling most of the work. This has helped them keep the fare on par with other vehicles, despite additional features like SMS for the hearing impaired and so on. Discount packages are offered for long weekends and special occasions, like any other cab service. Wheel-chair users, who work in India's Silicon Valley, gush over the fact that life has become easier now. The key to breaking even, however, is for the industry to avail of this service. Hospitals need to tie-up with them for rehabilitation services and companies need to tie-up for ferrying their disabled employees. Several enquiries have come in from Chennai and this will be the next city, for launching the disabled-friendly cab service.

Vidhya's first brush with disability was in a community project in Ladakh. Though the disabled population is small, they are visible and the community accepts their presence in a passive manner. Her grass-root work involved moving from village to village, trying to address the needs of a disabled person comprehensively – including linking children and adults to school, health services and finally, government benefits. She met Iqbal; a thirty year old disabled man, who could not go to school and yet was bright and motivated enough to make a difference. He suggested that they start a movement – One aimed at advocacy of disabled rights. As a result, Vidhya worked with him to set up a not-for-profit organisation called PAGIR. Besides advocacy, PAGIR worked on two livelihood initiatives – One was a waste to resources unit, which collected textiles and other waste material; recycling them into products for sale. 'Ladakh had no history of waste. Everything was consumed either by the humans or the animals. But with tourist inflow and consumerist packaged life, waste management has become a huge problem with little local knowledge of handling or managing this waste. So we thought of collecting this waste and linking it to livelihoods,' she expanded.

The other livelihood project set up in 2011 was the unique Himalaya-on-Wheels. It was planned to be a travel company like any other, but go the extra mile for the disabled, by recommending them accessible hotels and tourist sites. This meant that the PAGIR team had to first do an access audit of the hotels and the sightseeing places. Further, they had to suggest simple solutions like ramps; wherever possible. There are two challenges which Himalaya–on-Wheels is grappling with. Many tourist sites, like monasteries are steep and modifications are not possible. Also, the number of people with disability, wanting to travel to Ladakh was smaller than they had envisaged. Hence, the overall viability of the venture was a cause of concern.

From tackling inclusive transport in the mountains to the roads of Bangalore – it has definitely been a long journey for Vidhya. The decade long experience shall ensure, that this initial kickstart will pave a longer route to success, ensuring that the growing disabled community commutes comfortably.

ADVICE TO OTHERS

1. Entrepreneurs should first believe that it is important to have a disability focus – that diversity is important for a positive environment.
2. Help others in the workplace, to understand the importance of inter-dependency.
3. Ensure reasonable accommodation for those who require it.

Acknowledgements

I would like to thank the Fetzer Institute, USA, for their generosity in making this book possible. In particular Sharif Azami and Tiffany Jackson who coordinated our partnership.

Prasad Kaipa, has been a valued guide and mentor for Youth4Jobs and thus a natural collaborator.

I deeply value the time spent by each and every one interviewed for sharing their inspiring lives. Some of the stories are in this book; others have been retained for possible future use. Several people helped us along the way to implement the vision of the book. Friends like George Abraham and Shashi Baliga made useful suggestions.

I wanted to showcase the talent of the speech and hearing impaired youth and use sketches drawn by them rather than photographs. Thanks Smriti Nagpal and Atulyakala for bringing magic to paper through sketches which capture the uniqueness of each person profiled.

A special thanks to Niren Chaudhary who unhesitatingly introduced me to the publishers,

Bloomsbury. Praveen Tiwari of Bloomsbury who immediately understood the vision of the book, and kept insisting all along to have faith in him. Our editor, Ruchhita Kazaria, is now a friend. Chosen carefully by the publisher, she said she fell in love with the manuscript, and made sure the stories retained the narrators' voice. Thanks to Arunima Roy for marketing this special book in a special way. Snigdha Ehm and Sumant Agnihotri helped in early editing. Anila Mathur, Gopal Garg, Tapan Das and the Youth4Jobs team gave me space to escape and write and I am grateful for this. Sunita Singh for being my gracious hostess in Delhi. My friends, Amita Talwar and Raghu Cidambi for always being there. Shreedhar, Suchitra & Subodh at home, Premi and Ramakrishna in Chennai who believed in me; Anandi, Shankar, Siya and Mayee who gave me the quiet beauty of California to complete the book – a big thank you. Last but not least, thanks to the higher Force who is nameless, but guides silently in this journey.

Meera Shenoy

I appreciate all the support given by Sharif Azami and Fetzer Institute for making this project successful. I also appreciate the kind support of the business advisory group which allowed me to identify Youth 4 Jobs as an exemplar and have the opportunity to work with wonderful Meera Shenoy and her foundation. I always come away inspired after every meeting and visit with Meera.

Finally, Meera also deserves the credit for identifying the entrepreneurs and conducting interviews. This book truly would not have happened without all the hard work of Meera Shenoy.

Personally, I am grateful for the support of my wife Vinoda and continuous guidance given by my parents and Dr. Mohan Rao.

Prasad Kaipa

MEERA SHENOY

Meera Shenoy is a pioneer in skilling underprivileged youth, who has worked in senior positions in the government, in private sector and multilateral agencies like the World Bank and UNDP. Her work has demonstrated that skilling youth and placing them in jobs, can be done on a large scale, both for non-disabled rural youth and for youth with disability. Meera Shenoy is currently Founder-Chairperson of Youth4Jobs which focuses on helping companies build an inclusive workforce. Her recent work has won several awards, both national and international. She is often invited by management forums

About the Authors

to talk on integrating compassion and happiness in business. She has worked in the corporate sector, print media and television, and integrates this experience in her current work.

PRASAD KAIPA

Prasad is a visiting professor at the Indian School of Business (ISB) and was the founding Executive Director of the Center for Leadership, Innovation and Change (CLIC). He is the CEO of the Kaipa Group in California and works with companies and

C-suite executives in the areas of innovation, transformation and leadership development. He was a Smith Richardson Visiting Fellow at the Center for Creative Leadership in 2010–11. Prasad co-founded the Entrepreneur Institute for TiE (The Indus Entrepreneurs) in 2002 to help entrepreneurs connect their innovative ideas, products and services with effective ways to engage and co-create with others in the ecosystem. Prasad is co-author of a best-selling book "From Smart to Wise: Acting and Leading with Wisdom".